SYRIA
in Pictures

Alison Behnke

Lerner Publications Company

Contents

Lerner Publications Company
A division of Lerner Publishing Group
241 First Avenue North
Minneapolis, MN 55401 U.S.A.

Website address: www.lernerbooks.com

Library of Congress Cataloging-in-Publication Data

Behnke, Alison.
    Syria in pictures / by Alison Behnke.
       p.   cm. — (Visual geography series)
    Includes bibliographical references and index.
    ISBN: 0-8225-2396-5 (lib. bdg. : alk. paper)
    1. Syria—Juvenile literature. I. Title. II. Series.
DS93.B44 2005
956.91—dc22   2004014793

Manufactured in the United States of America
1 2 3 4 5 6 - BP - 10 09 08 07 06 05

INTRODUCTION

The Syrian Arab Republic lies at the eastern end of the Mediterranean Sea. Situated in a strategic location at the gateway between the Mediterranean region and the Middle East (a loosely defined area of southwestern Asia and North Africa), it has always drawn travelers to its shores. For many centuries, Syria has been a site of trade, cultural exchange, and numerous invasions. Among the land's many historical conquerors were the Greeks, the Romans, the Arabs, European crusaders, Ottoman Turks, and the French. But even amid these invasions, Syria has been home to grand and thriving civilizations.

Because so many outsiders have made Syria their home in the past, modern Syria has a varied heritage. Its population includes Arab and Kurdish ethnic groups, and the Islamic, Jewish, and Christian religions. This blend has given the small nation a rich combination of peoples. However, many Syrians cling to their regional, family, or religious loyalties rather than to a national identity, and so the country's diversity has also sometimes led to disunity and conflict.

Syria has long played a powerful role in the Middle East. For example, after achieving independence from France in 1946, Syria temporarily united with Egypt—then one of the most influential nations in the region. Since the mid-1970s, Syrian forces have been stationed in Lebanon, and Syrian leaders remain involved in Lebanese affairs. In addition, Syria has been actively involved in negotiations with Israel, a Middle Eastern nation that was created in 1948 as a Jewish homeland. The Palestinians, people living on land that became Israel, opposed the nation's existence. Some Palestinians turned to using terrorist tactics against Israel. Other nations accused Syria of supporting Palestinian terrorist organizations and their fight. Syria has consistently denied these charges, but it has nevertheless refused to accept peace agreements between Israel and the Arab world. A sticking point for Syria, in particular, is a region called the Golan Heights, which Israel claimed from Syria in a 1967 Arab-Israeli conflict.

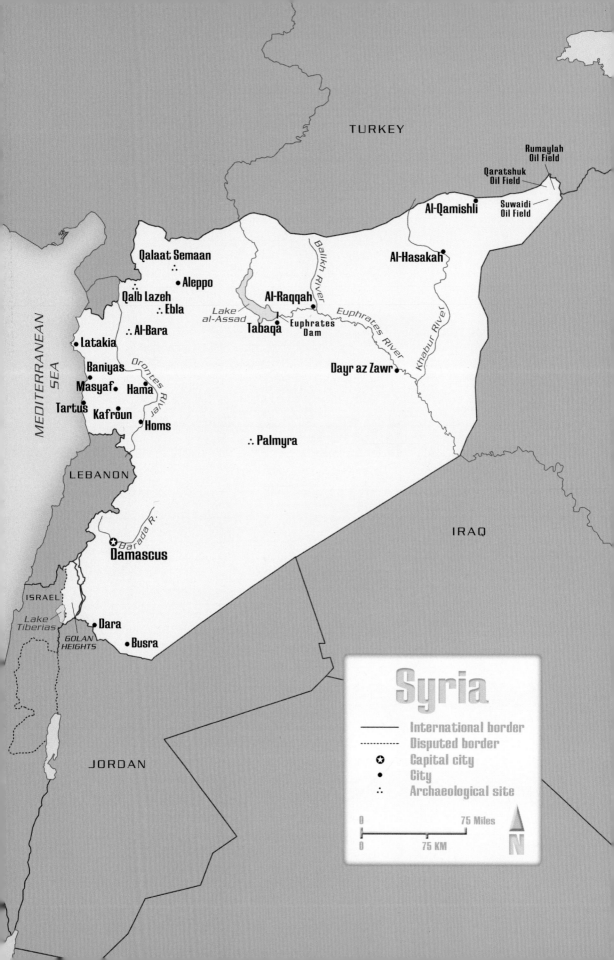

In 1971 General Hafez al-Assad took power in Syria as leader of the Baath political party. Although al-Assad brought nearly thirty years of relative stability to the nation, that stability often came at the expense of personal and political freedoms. After al-Assad's death in 2000, his son Bashar al-Assad took his father's place as the nation's leader. Taking office during a time of severe drought, small crop yields, rising foreign debt, and other challenges, Bashar al-Assad made promises to introduce many reforms. Real change has been slow in coming, however, and many observers are discouraged by the lack of significant reform to either social or economic policies.

Meanwhile, in 2001 international affairs overshadowed Syria's internal politics. Terrorist attacks on the United States led to new scrutiny of Syria's policies regarding terrorism in the Middle East. Then, in 2003, a U.S.-led war against Iraq brought even greater strife to the region and to Syria itself. Looking ahead, the nation's path to true political and economic stability may be a rocky one. But Syria has a long history of growth, change, and development. In addition, it has a rich culture, valued traditions, and a diverse and dynamic population. With such valuable resources to draw upon, Syria has great potential to reach its goals and to achieve the prosperity that it knew in ancient times.

THE LAND

Syria covers an area of 71,498 square miles (185,180 square kilometers), making it slightly larger than the U.S. state of Oklahoma. Turkey lies to the north, and Iraq is to the east. Jordan shares Syria's southern frontier, and Syria's western border skirts the Mediterranean Sea, Lebanon, and Israel.

The boundary between Syria and Israel has been in dispute since 1967. In that year, Israeli forces captured hills in southwestern Syria called the Golan Heights. The Israeli government made them part of Israel in 1981, but Syria still claims the Golan Heights as part of its national territory.

◯ Topography

Syria has four main natural land features. A group of mountains running from north to south separates a coastal plain from the interior. East of the mountains lies a fertile plateau and beyond it is the Syrian Desert.

The country's narrow coastal plain extends along the
Mediterranean Sea for more than 70 miles (113 km), running to the
southwest from Turkey to Lebanon. North of the Syrian port of
Latakia, the shoreline tends to be rugged, with rocky cliffs. South of
the city, the landscape is more level. Because the coastal plain receives
some of the nation's most plentiful rainfall, the land is intensely
farmed and heavily populated.

Syria's mountains are concentrated in the west and south. Parallel to
the coastal strip is the Jabal al-Nusayriyah—a limestone range that
reaches its highest point, about 5,000 feet (1,524 meters), at the northern end of the mountain chain. East of this range lies the Great Rift
Valley (also called the Al-Ghab Depression), through which the Orontes
River flows. Millions of years ago, a giant, shifting crack deep in the
earth's crust created this trenchlike valley, which extends far southward
into Africa. South of the Jabal al-Nusayriyah is a narrow corridor—the
Homs Gap—which has long been a pathway for traders and invaders.

On the other side of the gap are the Anti-Lebanon Mountains, which mark the boundary between Lebanon and Syria. This chain boasts Mount Hermon, which lies on the border between the two countries and, towering at 9,232 feet (2,814 m), is the highest peak in Syria. The Anti-Lebanon Mountains gradually decrease in elevation until they reach the Golan Heights. In the southwest are the volcanic peaks of the Jabal al-Arab (formerly the Jabal Druze). The western slopes of these mountains receive enough rainfall to support planted farmland. Many Syrians who belong to the Druze religious sect live in this rocky area.

Eastern Syria consists chiefly of a grassy plateau and the Syrian Desert. The plateau, which has an average elevation of 2,000 feet (610 m), receives relatively little rain. However, irrigation systems carry water from rivers, streams, and lakes into the fields of the plateau, allowing farmers to raise much of Syria's food and livestock there.

The Syrian Desert, which extends into Iraq and Jordan, is a roughly triangular land feature. Syria's portion of the desert covers most of the nation's southeastern territory and is largely flat, sloping gently northeastward to the Euphrates River. Deep wadis (riverbeds that carry water only during the rainy season) cut through the desert and also lead to the Euphrates.

◐ Rivers

Syria's most important waterways are the Euphrates (called Al-Furat in Syria) and the Orontes rivers. The 2,235-mile-long (3,597 km) Euphrates flows southeastward from its source in Turkey through a broad stretch of Syria. Cutting across the northeastern section of Syria's plateau, the waterway helps to create Al-Jazira—the upper part of the Tigris-Euphrates River valley, which stretches into Iraq.

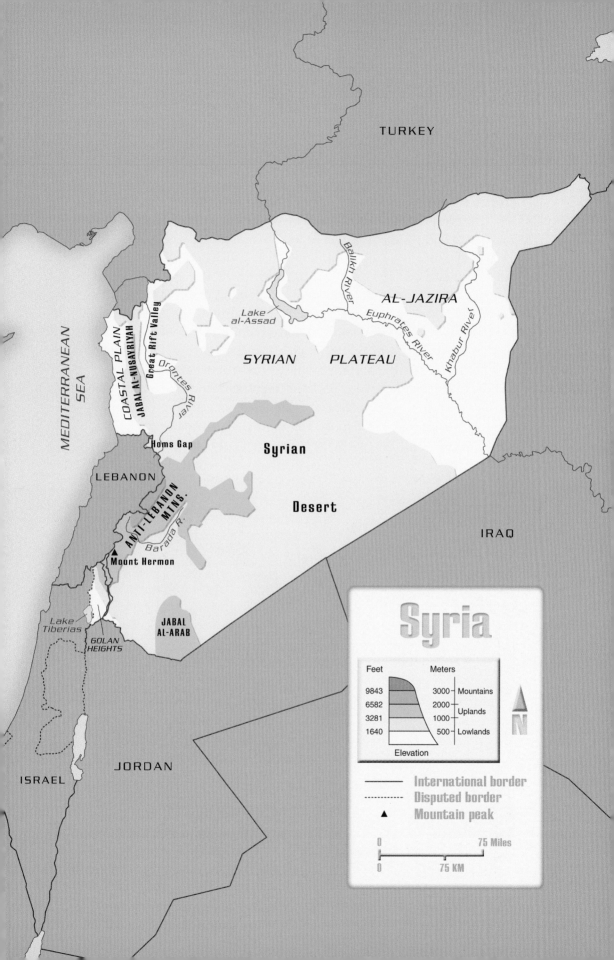

The Euphrates also forms the northeastern boundary of the Syrian Desert and eventually travels through Iraq to the Persian Gulf.

As the Euphrates winds through Syria, the river waters farmland and receives the volume of two branch rivers—the Balikh and the Khabur. The huge Euphrates Dam at Tabaqa uses the river's water to irrigate vast areas of once-uncultivated land. This engineering feat also created Lake al-Assad, a 30-mile-long (48 km) reservoir. The Euphrates also provides hydropower (water-generated electricity), and plans are in place to harness the power of other Syrian rivers as well.

The Orontes River flows for 355 miles (571 km), beginning near Baalbek, Lebanon, and entering Syria south of the city of Homs. Dams at Homs and Hama have rechanneled the Orontes to irrigate the surrounding countryside. Thanks to the Orontes River, harvests in western Syria are abundant, and local industries have hydropower to run their operations. After passing through northwestern Syria, the river enters Turkey and then empties into the Mediterranean Sea.

One other river—the Barada—is of importance to Syria. Beginning in the Anti-Lebanon Mountains, the Barada flows through the capital city of Damascus to the desert. The river provides water to the Al-Ghuta Oasis, a fertile area where the capital stands. And although

The famous old waterwheels in Hama are up to 90 feet (27 m) in diameter. They bring up water from the Orontes River for use in irrigation.

the dry season reduces the river to only a trickling stream, the Barada has allowed Damascus to be inhabited for thousands of years.

Climate

The climate of Syria varies greatly from west to east. Population centers and crop farming occur in places where rainfall is plentiful or where irrigation projects exist. In dry zones, nomads (people who move from place to place rather than living in permanent homes) commonly raise livestock, traveling wherever the grazing land is best for their flocks.

Although Mediterranean breezes cool the coastal plain, summers (May through August) in this region are generally hot and humid, with temperatures in the eighties and nineties. In winter (November through February), temperatures along the coast range between 48°F (9°C) and 68°F (20°C).

Life in the Syrian Desert can be brutal. Temperatures range over great extremes, from summer highs of 110°F (43°C) down to winter temperatures of about 35°F (2°C). During the long dry summer, hot winds stir up blinding sandstorms and dust storms that block vision and reshape the sand dunes.

Jabal al-Nusayriyah and the Anti-Lebanon Mountains act as a wall to moisture-carrying winds that blow in from the Mediterranean. As a result, the western slopes of these ranges are wetter and cooler than the eastern elevations. Temperature readings in the western mountains average about 72°F (22°C) in summer and 40°F (4°C) in winter. At the highest altitudes, temperatures frequently drop below freezing (32°F or 0°C) in the winter. East of the mountains, the plateau is semiarid, with hot summers and cool winters. Temperatures can climb to 104°F (40°C) in the summer, and winter levels drop below 45°F (7°C).

Syria's rainy season lasts from November to March. Rainfall is heaviest along the coast and in the mountain ranges that flank the coastal strip. In these areas, annual precipitation varies from 20 to 40 inches (51 to 102 centimeters) and may exceed 50 inches (127 cm) in some places. The highest elevations receive a portion of their moisture as snow.

Because the mountains keep most of the rain from entering the interior, the rest of Syria is nearly dry. The plateau that lies east of the mountains annually receives about 10 inches (25 cm) of rain. The desert may average as little as 3 inches (7.6 cm) per year. During very dry periods, it may not receive any precipitation at all.

Flora and Fauna

Syrians have so thoroughly cleared the coastal plain for farming and housing that not much of the original vegetation survives. Scrubby Mediterranean plants, such as tamarisk and buckthorn, grow in some of these cleared lands, and bright wildflowers thrive as weeds in cultivated fields.

Forests of oak and pine flourish in the northern part of the Jabal al-Nusayriyah, and hardwood trees cover the southern part of the same range. Thin stands of oak, pine, cedar, and cypress survive in the upper elevations of the Anti-Lebanon Mountains. On the grassy plains, terebinth trees are common. A member of the sumac family, this tree is an ancient source of turpentine (an oil used as paint thinner).

Human settlement has also decreased the habitats (natural homes) of Syria's wild mammals. Nevertheless, deer and gazelles continue to live in less populated areas. Rodents—such as dormice, squirrels, and rats—also make their homes in Syria. Other small mammals include hares, hedgehogs, wildcats, weasels, and foxes. Lions and leopards once roamed Syria, but bears are the only large mammals still reported. Among native birds are hawks, kites, cormorants, pelicans, flamingos, cuckoos, and woodpeckers. Desert animals include lizards and chameleons, as well as the sheep and camels of nomadic herders.

The **gazelle** is a longtime inhabitant of the lands of Syria. Gazelles can survive with very little water, making them well suited to Syria's dry climate.

Natural Resources and Environmental Challenges

Petroleum (oil) is Syria's most important natural resource, but the nation's oil deposits are small compared to those of some other Middle Eastern states. First discovered in Syria in the 1950s, petroleum has grown into the nation's leading national export. Most of Syria's oil fields lie in the northeastern part of the country.

After oil, Syria's chief resources are natural gas, phosphates, iron ore, salt, and asphalt. These substances exist in large enough quantities to be mined profitably. Smaller amounts of coal, copper, lead, and gold have been discovered in mountain areas.

Syria lacks other important resources, however, such as arable (farmable) land, adequate water, and timber. The overuse of these resources has resulted in a number of serious environmental issues. Deforestation is a major challenge, as Syria's trees are harvested at a quick pace to be used as building material. Deforestation leads, in turn, to erosion, as the lack of protection by forest cover allows precious topsoil to be swept away by rain and wind. Desertification is another related problem, in which land that has been deforested and overgrazed gradually turns from arable land to desert.

In addition, Syria's limited water supply has suffered from pollution and overuse. Air pollution, especially near Damascus, is also a threat to the environment. These problems have endangered Syrian wildlife, as well, such as the once-populous Syrian bear and the Mediterranean monk seal, which may already be extinct in Syria.

Since the mid-1990s, the Syrian government has taken steps to address these problems. The nation has signed several international environmental agreements and has implemented programs to plant new trees. Successful reforestation will help prevent further desertification. Nevertheless, the country's precious resources and environmental health are still at risk.

Cities

About half of Syria's 18 million people live in urban areas, most of which are concentrated in the west, where rainfall is relatively plentiful. Syria's cities and towns have long histories and feature narrow streets, ancient buildings, and traditional ways of life. Most large urban centers have added modern housing and business districts to accommodate their growing number of residents.

DAMASCUS is the nation's capital and, with an estimated population of more than 1.6 million people, its largest city. Damascus serves as Syria's hub of business, government, and communications. Situated

Damascus, the capital and chief city of Syria, has long been an important commercial center.

between the Anti-Lebanon Mountains and the Syrian Desert, Damascus lies in the Al-Ghuta Oasis—a triangular network of irrigation canals fed by the Barada River.

Located along the route between Europe, the Middle East, and eastern Asia, Damascus has been a commercial center since ancient times. The capital's colorful streets, once crowded with traders from around the world, are still filled with people—as well as trucks, cars, and buses. Merchants sell food, fabrics, and metalwork in markets called souks.

Ancient Damascus lies on the southern bank of the Barada River, while modern Damascus extends north of the Barada and boasts wide avenues, large apartment buildings, and tall office complexes. The business district took shape during the early 1900s, when France controlled Syria. Many of the city's institutions—such as the National Museum and the National Library—preserve Syria's cultural diversity. The capital's manufacturing sector produces textiles and processed food. Damascus University sits on the outskirts of the capital.

ALEPPO, located in northwestern Syria, is the nation's second-largest city with more than one million inhabitants. Like Damascus, Aleppo has a long history. Archaeological evidence suggests that people may have settled in the area before 5000 B.C. Aleppo has many historic and religious sites including a large twelfth-century Arab fort. Standing on a bluff that dominates the older part of the city, the fort has beautiful tiled ceilings and strong walls. Shops that offer a wide variety of goods line Aleppo's vast network of souks. Included in the trading district are traditional public baths and khans—ancient resting places for caravan travelers.

Modern Aleppo is a commercial and industrial hub and a marketplace for farmers from surrounding regions. The city's chief industries are textile manufacturing, tobacco refining, and food processing, mainly of dried fruits and nuts. The nearby Euphrates Dam—which has enabled farmers to grow large amounts of wheat, barley, and cotton—has helped increase Aleppo's importance.

HOMS, with 430,000 people, lies along a route between Damascus and Aleppo in west central Syria. Situated on the Orontes River, the city was once the center of the worship of Baal, a sun god of ancient times. Set amid one of the most fertile areas of Syria, Homs is famous for silk manufacturing and contains large oil-refining facilities.

HAMA (population 200,000) was settled long before 1000 B.C. Built on the banks of the Orontes River, the city lies in a district where farmers plant large fields of grain and cotton. In the sixteenth century, enormous waterwheels were built in Hama to pump water from the Orontes to nearby farmland. Some of the wheels are up to 90 feet (27 m) in diameter. In modern times, the city's main industries are food processing and the manufacture of clothing and carpets.

LATAKIA (population 240,000), the chief seaport of Syria, survived through the rule of Phoenicians, Assyrians, Babylonians, Greeks, and Romans. The modern city bears traces of these centuries of outside control. Latakia's Roman ruins, which include the Temple of Bacchus and the Triumphal Arch, are among the finest ancient sites in Syria. As a result of its seaside location, Latakia benefits from Mediterranean breezes that soften the extremes of the region's summer and winter temperatures. The hub of the Syrian tobacco industry, Latakia also exports cotton, asphalt, and foodstuffs. A leading resort, the city draws visitors to its beaches and historical sites.

Visit www.vgsbooks.com where you will find links to more information about Syria's cities—including what there is to see and do, the climate and weather, and more.

HISTORY AND GOVERNMENT

The ancient territory known as Greater Syria once included a much larger area than the modern Syrian Arab Republic encompasses. At different times in history, land that later became Lebanon, Jordan, Israel, and parts of Turkey and Iraq belonged to Greater Syria.

Livestock herders are thought to have lived in the region as early as 5000 B.C. They led a nomadic lifestyle, moving from place to place with the herds and the seasons rather than forming permanent settlements. Almost all of these inhabitants were Semitic peoples, whose ancestors originated in the Arabian Peninsula to the south. Later, Greater Syria's rich farmland drew many other groups to the area.

▶ Early History

The earliest archaeological evidence of Syria's ancient inhabitants comes from a site at Ebla. Excavations of this city in northern Syria show that a large-scale Semitic culture flourished there in about 2500 B.C. Ebla was a commercial center that linked Anatolia (modern

Turkey), the Tigris-Euphrates River valley (in present-day Iraq), and Persia (modern-day Iran).

For several centuries, Ebla struggled against Akkad—a kingdom in the southern Tigris-Euphrates Valley—for control of the region's trade routes. In about 2250 B.C., the Akkadian king, Naram-Sin, defeated the armies of Ebla and burned the city to the ground.

Meanwhile, a Semitic people called the Amorites had arrived from the Arabian Peninsula in 2400 B.C. In time, they also became targets for Akkadian forces. Yet despite Akkadian attacks, the Amorites stayed in the region. A branch of this group of people, the Canaanites, eventually occupied Greater Syria's Mediterranean coast (in present-day Lebanon).

Lying near the intersection of Africa, Asia, and Europe, Syria became an even more important hub of agricultural and commercial activity. Syria's coastal location attracted traders from all over the Middle East in large numbers. The area's residents developed into expert shipbuilders and sailors, and their seafaring activities linked Syria to many new Mediterranean trading centers. By about 1800 B.C., these sailors became known as Phoenicians.

FALL OF PALMYRA

In the third century A.D., the Syrian city of Palmyra was the capital of a powerful semi-independent kingdom. It was also a trading center for the caravans of camels and carts that wound their way from Homs to settlements along the Euphrates. But when the Palmyrenes resisted Rome's rule, Emperor Aurelian attacked in A.D. 272. When a second revolt broke out the following year, Aurelian returned and destroyed the city. As one historian describes it, "Aurelian besieged [Palmyra]... and Palmyra had no choice but to surrender. The conqueror despoiled it of its rich fabrics and precious ornaments, some of which were taken to embellish the new sun temple at Rome.... Palmyra fell into insignificance and obscurity; as its people relaxed their grip on the desert, the desert overcame them."

—Philip K. Hitti, *Syria: A Short History* (1959)

To learn more about Palmyra, visit www.vgsbooks.com.

New Foreign Influences

The Egyptians and the Hittites (a people from Anatolia) extended control over portions of Syria at various times during the next several hundred years. Toward the end of the eleventh century B.C., two Semitic peoples—the Hebrews and the Aramaeans—became influential in the region.

The Hebrews introduced the local people to the religious idea of monotheism (belief in one god), and their beliefs eventually grew into early Judaism. Aramaean merchants made Damascus a center for overland commercial routes to southern Arabia and Persia. As Aramaean traders traveled in the Middle East, they spread their language—Aramaic—throughout the area. Aramaic eventually became the principal language of Syria.

Between the 1000s and the 500s B.C., Syria was controlled for brief periods by different foreign neighbors. From the sixth to the fourth centuries B.C., the land was part of the Persian Empire centered in modern Iran. In 333 B.C., Alexander the Great and his Greek armies conquered the vast Persian realm, and it was from the Greeks that the region got the name Syria. After Alexander died, Syria came under the authority of one of his generals, named Seleucus.

Seleucus founded a family of rulers known as the Seleucid dynasty, which governed Syria for three centuries. The Seleucid leaders made their capital in Damascus and brought elements of ancient Greek culture and religion to Syria. The Syrians combined Greek ideas with their own learning to make advances in science, architecture, and philosophy. During this period, the Syrians built many roads and cities, and traders established commercial routes into Europe and India.

In the first century B.C., the Armenians and the Parthians—peoples from the north and east—began to expand their holdings by invading Syrian territory. These groups did not control the region for long, however. In 64 B.C., Syria became part of the vast Roman Empire, which was based in Italy but had conquered parts of North Africa and Asia. The period of Roman rule in Syria was generally prosperous. Roman administrators built roads, temples, and aqueducts (structures that carry water over long distances). Following Rome's adoption of Christianity as its official religion in the early A.D. 300s, Syria was also exposed to the new religion. Damascus remained prominent under Roman rule, and the city became famous for its architecture and its schools of law and medicine.

In 395 the Roman Empire split into two portions. Syria became part of the Eastern Roman, or Byzantine, Empire. Byzantine emperors governed the territory from the city of Constantinople (which later became Istanbul, Turkey). Under the empire, Christianity continued to spread, especially in northern Syria.

Over the next several centuries, the Byzantine Empire was often at war with Persia. Syria frequently became a battlefield, and the fighting drained Constantinople's finances. As the Byzantine Empire's hold on the region weakened, invaders from the Arabian Peninsula met little resistance as they moved toward southern Syria in the early 600s.

Islam and the Arabs

In the early seventh century, the Arab prophet Muhammad founded a new faith called Islam. By 629 his followers, called Muslims, set out from their capital at Mecca on the Arabian Peninsula to establish Islam in other lands. Soon after the death of Muhammad in 632, Muslims divided into two main sects. Sunni Muslims favored electing their leader, while Shiites wanted Islam's head to be chosen from among Muhammad's family. Sunnis became Islam's dominant group.

Led by Khalid ibn al-Walid, Islamic forces conquered Damascus in 636. Under Islamic rule, Syria slowly adopted Islam as its official religion. Muawiyah I, a Sunni who belonged to the Umayyad family, became Syria's caliph (Islamic ruler). In 661 his followers elected him leader of all Muslims, and he chose Damascus as his political capital.

Muawiyah I and other Umayyad caliphs extended the Islamic Empire westward to Spain and eastward to central Asia. But the empire's leadership was unstable. Later, Umayyad caliphs moved away from Islamic traditions, and in 715 the Abbasids, a rival Muslim family, overthrew the Umayyad dynasty. The Abbasids transferred the capital of the empire from Damascus to Baghdad (in present-day Iraq).

In time, however, the Abbasids also began to ignore Islamic traditions, and their power over the Islamic Empire weakened. By the 1000s, when Turkish forces invaded the region, Syria had already split into several small Islamic states. The Turks—who, like the Abbasids, were Muslims—conquered Syria and established two provinces with capitals at Aleppo and Damascus. Turkish control eventually made it difficult for European Christians to travel to Palestine, a Middle Eastern land that Christians, Muslims, and Jews all considered sacred. To make safe passage possible—and to gain control of the region's riches—Christian armies arrived from western Europe in the late eleventh century.

Known as crusaders, these Christian soldiers fought to take Palestine in a series of wars known as the Crusades. They conquered Turkish territory and set up centers at Antioch (in Anatolia), Tripoli (in Greater Syria), and Jerusalem (in Palestine). The Syrian cities of Damascus, Homs, and Hama, however, remained under Turkish authority.

Krak des Chevaliers, the most famous medieval citadel in the world, was built by the crusaders near the present-day city of Homs.

In the early 1100s, ongoing warfare against the crusaders broke the power of the Turks in Syria. Zangi, a Muslim noble from Mosul (in modern Iraq), defeated a number of both crusaders and Turks, pushing them out of northern Syria. Zangi's son, Nureddin, succeeded his father and moved the capital of his growing kingdom first to Aleppo and then to Damascus.

Soon after taking power, Nureddin was asked by an Egyptian leader for help with internal disputes and attacks from crusaders. In 1169 Nureddin sent one of his armies to Egypt, led by his skilled general Saladin. Saladin soon became influential in the Egyptian administration and took control of Egypt in 1171. After Nureddin's death in 1174, Saladin became sultan of both Egypt and Syria.

DRAWN TO DAMASCUS

As the hub of the growing Islamic Empire, Damascus enjoyed a period of fame and wealth. Meanwhile, the entire empire flourished and developed. Under the influence of Islam, Syrians substituted Arabic for Aramaic as the main language of the Middle East. The rulers of Syria built roads, founded hospitals, and encouraged education. Scholars from other lands studied in Damascus, developing new medical practices and philosophical ideas.

Saladin was able to bring the armies of several Muslim nobles under his control, and he used his newly unified forces to push the crusaders out of Jerusalem in 1188. However, Muslim and Christian forces in other parts of the Middle East continued to fight until 1192, when the two groups finally agreed to a truce. The agreement allowed Christians to have access to Jerusalem in Palestine and to establish a limited number of outposts on Syria's coast.

Mongols, Mamluks, and Ottomans

After Saladin's death in 1192, Syria again broke into several states. In 1260 the Mongols, warriors from central Asia, invaded Syria, killing thousands of people and destroying mosques (Islamic places of worship), homes, and aqueducts. Mongol attacks on Syria in the thirteenth and fourteenth centuries met retaliation from the Mamluk dynasty, which had established itself in Egypt in 1250. By the 1300s, Mamluk forces had claimed the region as part of their kingdom. Despite repeated Mongol raids, the Mamluks founded a prosperous realm. But the most destructive Mongol attack came in 1402, when Timur the Lame (also called Tamerlane) captured and plundered Damascus.

Syria did not easily recover from the damage inflicted by Timur and his troops. The Mamluks continued to rule the area, but they became less and less effective. In 1516 the Ottoman Turks, founders of a new Islamic Empire in central Asia, defeated the Mamluks and began a three-hundred-year rule of Syria. The Ottomans eventually controlled a section of southeastern Europe, most of southwestern Asia, and part of northern Africa.

The Ottomans ruled through pashas—leaders who were given complete authority over their areas. The pashas employed local civic and religious officials to collect taxes, establish courts, and govern communities. Under the pashas' control, heavy taxes, inefficient management, and diminished trade hampered Syria's growth. By the late 1700s, Syria's thriving economy and culture seemed to be things of the past.

European Intervention

As Syria slipped into decline, new developments affected its future. As the Ottoman Empire weakened, European powers took a growing interest in the Middle East. Hoping to expand their holdings and trade routes, Europeans saw great commercial possibilities in Syria and hoped to gain control of the strategically located territory.

European powers soon played a different role in local affairs. In the 1800s, tensions began to rise between Maronites (Christians in Greater Syria who were part of a division of the Roman Catholic Church) and the Druze, members of a religion that had grown out of Islam in the eleventh century. Competition over social and economic status grew between the two religious groups. In 1860 these tensions erupted into violence when Druze fighters attacked the Maronites, killing an estimated ten thousand people or more. The French, who had developed ties with the Maronites, sent troops to intervene and forced the Ottomans to establish a new, semi-independent province for the Maronites. This Christian-governed realm was carved out of Greater Syria and eventually would evolve into modern-day Lebanon.

This European involvement stirred up the region. Many Syrians had grown restless with the increasingly inefficient Ottoman rule and with its burdensome policies, such as high taxes and the drafting of young Syrian men into the Ottoman army. In response to complaints, Ottoman officials attempted reforms. However, their changes met with limited success, and Syrian demands for relief rose. Despite Ottoman attempts to suppress unrest, by the beginning of the twentieth century, an Arab independence movement had taken hold in Syria and other Middle Eastern nations.

⊙ War and Division

Just as the Arab movement toward self-rule gained momentum, World War I (1914–1918) broke out. During this large-scale conflict, Syrian soldiers fought in battles that pitted Britain, France, and Russia against Germany and Ottoman Turkey. British officials and Arab nobles seeking further help in defeating the Ottomans turned to Hussein ibn Ali, the head of an influential Arab family. Led by Hussein's son Faisal, Arab forces launched their first attack in 1916. With the assistance of British officer T. E. Lawrence, Arab troops took Damascus in 1918. Faisal became military governor, and the Ottomans were defeated that same year. Also in 1918, Germany's surrender ended the war.

Most Syrians and other Arab soldiers who fought in the war expected the European victors to help build independent Arab states out of formerly Ottoman territory. In preparation for self-government, Syrians organized a national congress that elected Faisal king of Syria, which at that time included Palestine and Transjordan (modern-day Jordan). Syrian leaders also began to write an Arabic-language constitution.

However, France and Britain were both eager to maintain influence in the Middle East—especially as they believed that the region might hold valuable oil reserves. As a result, they refused to recognize Syria as an independent nation. The French government blocked Faisal and sought to establish a mandate (decree of legal control) over Syria.

France and Britain ultimately decided how to divide the Arab territories and who would control them. The basis for these decisions was the Sykes-Picot Agreement, a document secretly signed by representatives of the British and French governments. Despite Faisal's protests, the Europeans carried out the agreement's terms stating that France would rule Syria and Lebanon, while Britain would have authority over Palestine, Transjordan, and Iraq. The French mandate in Syria began on July 15, 1920, and Faisal left the country. The French divided Syria into several areas

LIBERATION OF DAMASCUS

"When dawn came we drove to the head of the ridge, which stood over the oasis of the city, afraid to look north for the ruins we expected: but, instead of ruins, the silent gardens stood blurred green with river mist in whose setting shimmered the city, beautiful as ever, like a pearl in the morning sun."

—T. E. Lawrence, describing the morning after German forces were unexpectedly defeated and driven from Damascus during World War I

and administered them through a French high commissioner in Beirut, the capital of Lebanon.

This decision by outsiders to split Arab territory and place it under European control led to deep bitterness and anti-European feeling in the Middle East. Arab nationalism grew, as did pan-Arabism—a movement that aimed to establish a single Arab state in the region. Hostilities continued to build over the next twenty-five years, as the French censored newspapers, imposed the French language in schools, and refused to set a timetable for eventual self-rule.

In 1925 Syrians revolted against French control. French troops put down the rebellion with great force, but by 1939 Syrian dissatisfaction had mounted again, when France gave Turkey control over Alexandretta, a northwestern district claimed by Arab nationalists.

A **Syrian rebel caravan** carries away loot from a four-day siege on a city that was defended by the French in December 1925.

World War II (1939–1945) broke out that same year, and Syrians were more eager than ever to escape European rule.

World War II once again pitted France, Britain, and their allies against Germany, which at that time was led by the Nazi Party. In 1940 France fell to Nazi forces, giving the Germans the power to appoint the French high commissioner of Syria. But in 1941, soldiers from Britain, Jordan, and Free France (an anti-German French resistance movement) overthrew the new administration in Syria. Free French authorities took over, and the group's leader—General Charles de Gaulle—promised that Syria would eventually win self-rule. By the time the war ended in 1945, France's allies—the Soviet Union, the United States, and Great Britain—had formally recognized Syrian independence. Nevertheless, France still clung to control over the colony, maintaining French troops on Syrian soil.

Independence and the Search for Unity

Following World War II, de Gaulle, as leader of the new French government, began to resist the Syrian drive for independence. In May 1945, Syrians protested against the ongoing French presence again, staging demonstrations in the streets of Damascus, Aleppo, Homs, and Hama. Fighting erupted in the capital, and the French bombed the city. In response, Britain threatened to send troops into Syria against France. The United Nations (UN, an international peacekeeping organization) also pressured France to recognize Syria's independence. On April 17, 1946, the French finally evacuated their troops, and Syria was a fully self-governing republic at last.

The new country faced many difficulties, including changing politics in the Middle East. In 1948 the Jewish State of Israel was created from part of British-controlled Palestine. Many Arabs fiercely opposed this development, and that same year, Syria and other Arab countries attacked Israel in the hope of regaining what they regarded as Arab territory. When Israel won the war, many Syrians blamed their own leaders for the defeat and remained opposed to Israel's presence.

The loss of the 1948 war to Israeli forces added to growing instability within Syria's new independent government. The nation underwent three coups d'état (sudden overthrows of government) in 1949 alone. General Adib Shishakli—the leader of the third 1949 coup—seized control of the government and ruled as a military dictator for five years. In 1954 he was overthrown, and the officers who ousted him allowed a group of civilian politicians to form an administration.

A new political organization, the Baath Party, gained strength in the mid-1950s. Formed by Michel Aflaq, a Christian, and Salah al-

Din al-Bitar, a Sunni Muslim, the new party wanted to revive pan-Arabism and to introduce a socialist form of government to the region. (Socialism is a political and economic system that places all resources under government control, with the goal of dividing them equally among citizens.) After Shishakli's fall, a number of Baathists won seats in the national legislature and began to lay the foundation for their eventual rule in Syria.

The hopes of many Syrians for a united Arab nation became a reality in 1958. The pan-Arab movement had been gaining momentum for some time, and one of its strongest supporters was Egypt's president Gamal Abdel Nasser. Syrians turned to Nasser to lead a combined Syrian-Egyptian state known as the United Arab Republic (UAR).

Many Syrians, however, soon came to believe that power was unevenly shared by the two parts of the UAR. Egypt had a larger population, a more developed economy, and a more dynamic leader. In addition, the new nation's central administration was located in the Egyptian part of the country, and a large number of Egyptians gained high posts in the Syrian sector of the UAR.

The Arab union lasted only until 1961, when Syrian army officers seized control of their territory and withdrew from the UAR. The leaders of the revolt were primarily Alawis—members of an Islamic subgroup. Rejecting Aflaq and al-Bitar's leadership, they developed their own branch of the Baath Party. Less committed to Arab unity than their predecessors, these officers focused their attention on the economic development of Syria.

The Baath Party and Hafez al-Assad

Several factions of the Baath Party struggled for control of the country in the 1960s. Unrest returned, with ten coups—some of them violent—occurring between 1963 and 1970. Slowly, the Alawi general Hafez al-Assad and his followers began to gather strength in the Baath ranks. Baathists who had been overthrown left the country and lived in exile. Iraq gave refuge to some of these fleeing Baathists, creating tension between Syria and Iraq.

In June 1967, a new development in the ongoing Arab-Israeli conflict helped General al-Assad and his party gain wider support. That month Israeli troops defeated Egypt, Jordan, and Syria in a war that lasted six days. Israel gained a significant amount of Arab territory in the Six-Day War, including Syria's Golan Heights region. This loss—and the building of Israeli settlements there that followed—created even greater disunity in Syrian politics, as leaders blamed one another for the defeat. Al-Assad took advantage of the confusion to increase his power in Syria and in the region. He supported Palestinian refugees who had fled to Jordan from areas held by Israel. He also backed Palestinian efforts to form their own political forces, including the Palestine Liberation Organization (PLO). After coming into conflict with the Jordanian government in 1970, the PLO and other Palestinian groups moved into Lebanon and Syria.

Al-Assad extended support and funding to Palestinian groups, some of whom had adopted terrorist tactics against Israel. But he also placed those operating in Syria under close supervision from his military forces. Most Palestinians eventually moved into Lebanon, where they could receive weapons and money from Syria without directly being under Syrian control.

During Hafez al-Assad's years in office, Syrians saw him everywhere. Al-Assad's portrait hung in public buildings, homes, and streets, sometimes on banners or posters many feet high, and statues of him dotted Syrian cities.

This poster is typical of the portraits of **Hafez al-Assad** that are found throughout Syria.

Meanwhile, as these external changes occurred, al-Assad made his move to take power in Syria. In October 1970, his troops surrounded a meeting of Baath Party leaders and al-Assad took control of the party. In 1971 he became president of Syria, running as the only candidate in a national election.

Al-Assad's new government took over the holdings of many wealthy landowners, breaking the land into smaller plots and redistributing them to farmworkers. Al-Assad also strengthened his power by naming many of his fellow Alawis to high positions in the Baath Party and the Syrian government. These moves put him in conflict with the majority religious population of Sunni Muslims, who did not like al-Assad's strict control. But al-Assad's opponents faced the president's security forces, who used harsh measures including arrest, torture, and execution, to eliminate dissent. Under their control, freedom of speech and political activities of any kind were severely limited.

In 1973 Egypt and Syria joined in a surprise attack against Israel. Syrian forces at first regained part of the Golan Heights. But Israeli troops rallied to overcome Syrian forces, eventually occupying even more ground than they had claimed at the end of 1967. Only through negotiations at the end of the war did Syria finally get back a small part of the Golan Heights. Compared to other military encounters with Israel, however, Syrians considered the 1973 war a victory.

Entanglement in Lebanon

Following the 1973 war, Syria turned its attention from Israel to Lebanon. Over the years, Syrian leaders, including al-Assad, had often intervened in Lebanon's internal affairs, backing different—and even opposing—Lebanese groups to promote Syria's own interests in the region. This involvement grew even more complicated during a civil war in Lebanon, which erupted between the nation's Christians and Muslims in the mid-1970s. Several Syrian-supported Islamic factions entered the war. But in 1976, a Lebanese Christian faction asked Syria for help in stopping the conflict. Al-Assad responded by sending thousands of troops to Lebanon, and the Syrian army took control of portions of eastern and northern Lebanon.

While the move helped prevent Lebanon from completely breaking apart, Syria's military presence did not halt the violence. In some cases, Syria's presence even increased it. But the intervention did help serve al-Assad's own interests, as troops helped keep the Lebanese-Syrian border stable.

With its greater involvement in Lebanon, the Syrian government decided to increase Syria's military strength by obtaining more weapons. Throughout the 1980s, a steady supply of missiles arrived

Tanks carrying **Syrian soldiers** drive through Beirut, Lebanon, in 1987.

from the Soviet Union (present-day Russia and other republics), which had long been supplying Syria with arms. As the decade progressed, many Lebanese—especially Christians—began trying to oust the Syrians. In response, al-Assad and the Islamic militias that he supported only raised the intensity of the fighting.

Conflict Inside and Out

While Syria was embroiled in Lebanese affairs, its relations with Iraq also worsened. Although Baath Party leaders ran both countries, several issues—such as water rights and oil pipeline operations—divided the two nations.

These tensions led Syria to side with Iran during the Iran-Iraq War (1980–1988). This stance put Syria at odds with most Arab states of the Middle East, which supported Iraq, and some Arab nations decreased their financial aid to Syria as a result. Even following a UN-sponsored cease-fire that ended the war in August 1988, Syria's feud with Iraq continued. Iraq began to supply weapons to Lebanese Christian groups fighting Syria's militias in Lebanon.

Meanwhile, within Syria, anti-government unrest had grown. An extreme religious group called the Muslim Brotherhood was especially outspoken against al-Assad. Aiming to overthrow Syria's Baath government and replace it with Shiite Muslim leaders, the Brotherhood organized labor strikes, attacked Alawites (members of al-Assad's religion), and made assassination attempts on al-Assad himself. In 1982 these tensions exploded in an uprising in the city of Hama. Government forces moved in, besieging the city and forcefully crushing the rebellion. Much of Hama was destroyed, and the number of dead was estimated at 30,000 or more.

In August 1990, a new crisis emerged when Iraq invaded the small neighboring country of Kuwait. The UN condemned Iraq's actions, and in January 1991, many countries—including Syria and the United States—declared war on Iraq. This time, Syria's anti-Iraq stance was in line with most of the region's views. Syria provided both troops and weapons to the war effort, helping rebuild and improve the nation's relations with both the United States and other Western powers, as well as with its Arab neighbors. By March 1991, Iraq had been defeated in a relatively quick and decisive war, often called the Persian Gulf War.

In 1991 Syria and Lebanon also finally agreed to a formal cease-fire and a security pact that required Syria to move its troops to northeastern Lebanon. The peace agreement between Syria and Lebanon was welcomed by the international community. But many nations still had major concerns regarding Syria's ties to terrorism. The United States, Britain, and other countries had charged Syria with supporting Palestinian terrorism. Some also believed that Syria had influenced Islamic factions in Lebanon that had seized U.S. and European hostages. Although Syrian officials denied any connection with these events, the terrorism question remained.

◉ Old Troubles and New Wars

Meanwhile, Syria's negotiations with Israel over peace and the Golan Heights continued. A series of talks—many arranged or overseen by the United States—brought Syrian and Israeli officials together. Several tentative agreements emerged, such as a 1994 proposal that outlined a gradual process in which control over the Golan Heights would be returned to Syria over an eight-year period.

However, ongoing developments in regional politics led to uncertainty and conflict, and each new round of talks ended without significant progress. Violence also erupted periodically, with suicide bombings in Israel prompting new calls for al-Assad to oust *expel* Palestinian terrorist groups that operated from Syria. Syria also blamed several bombing incidents within its own country on Israel, although many observers doubted the charges. Renewed negotiations began in December 1999 in the United States, but they quickly ran into problems and were indefinitely postponed in January 2000.

At the same time, Syria's domestic issues were similarly bleak. Plagued by frequent droughts, falling export income, and decreased funds from other Arab states, the nation's economy had steadily declined over the previous decade. Then, on June 10, 2000, Hafez al-Assad died following a heart attack. Some observers worried that the death of this strong and decisive leader after so many years in power would throw the country into chaos. But, al-Assad's son Bashar al-Assad quickly emerged as his successor. Within just a few days of his father's burial, Bashar was nominated by the Baathists as the sole candidate for president, and on July 10, he was elected by the People's Assembly (the national legislature).

In June 2000, following Hafez al-Assad's death, the Syrian constitution was amended to lower the required age to be president from forty to thirty-four—Bashar al-Assad's exact age at the time.

Within just a few months of al-Assad's oath of office, the Israel situation once again loomed large. An uprising called the al-Aqsa Intifada broke out among Palestinians living in Israeli-held areas. Violence skyrocketed, as Palestinian terrorist groups carried out suicide bombings against Israel and as Israel retaliated with military assaults. Syria's decision to continue to allow Palestinian terrorists to take refuge within its borders and to launch attacks from its territory drew widespread criticism and further strained Syrian-Israeli relations. Meanwhile, Syria also felt international pressure to remove the twenty-five thousand troops it still had stationed in Beirut. Although Syria finally complied, it kept some of its forces in rural Lebanon.

On September 11, 2001, the Afghanistan-based terrorist group al-Qaeda carried out devastating terrorist attacks on the United States, flying planes into New York City's World Trade Center and the Pentagon near Washington, D.C. Following the attacks, a heightened international focus on terrorism and its sponsors brought new pressure on Syria. Although Syria joined the UN Security Council (a committee of the UN that monitors conflict) in October, U.S. leaders remained critical of what they called Syria's tolerance for terrorism.

Over the course of 2002, Syria also struggled with several internal disasters. In June a dam burst in northwestern Syria, killing twenty people, flooding three villages, and leaving approximately two thousand families homeless. In September a serious bus accident killed thirteen, and in October thirty-one lives were lost when five poorly built homes collapsed in Aleppo. But by early 2003, international

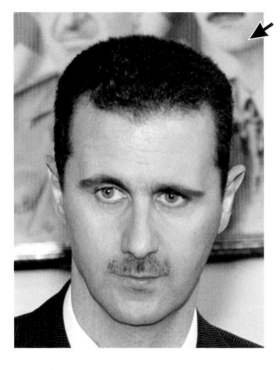

Bashar al-Assad has been Syria's president since the death of his father in 2000.

affairs took center stage once again. In March 2003, the United States led a war against Iraq over that nation's suspected possession of weapons of mass destruction (chemical, nuclear, or other weapons capable of killing large numbers of soldiers and civilians). The war was widely unpopular in the Middle East, and Syrian political and religious leaders were especially outspoken in denouncing the U.S.-led invasion.

Ongoing Challenges

While the Iraq war continued, Syria and Israel came into conflict yet again. In October 2003, Israeli forces bombed a site near Damascus that was suspected to be a Palestinian terrorist training camp. The bombings and Israel's proposal to create new settlements in the Golan Heights added fuel to the fire and attracted international criticism.

In 2004, however, Syria returned to the spotlight as the target of terrorism accusations. In May 2004, the United States placed economic sanctions (penalties) on Syria, charging that the nation continued to back terrorism and that it had sought to obtain weapons of mass destruction. U.S. officials also accused Syria of allowing terrorists and military supplies to cross back and forth over its border with Iraq, where U.S. forces were battling fierce attacks by rebels and Islamic terrorists.

In autumn 2004, Syria came under renewed pressure to leave Lebanon when the UN called for the removal of all foreign forces. With about fifteen thousand troops left in the Lebanese territory, Syria responded by repositioning—but not removing—its forces.

In addition to the many international issues facing Syria, citizens continue to confront challenges at home. Bashar al-Assad became president with pledges to modernize the government, to increase civil rights, and to crack down on government corruption. However, many people feel that his actions since taking office have not lived up to these promises. In the early years of al-Assad's term, many political prisoners were released, and governmental reorganization took place. But at the same time, freedom of speech and press remain limited, and citizens who speak out may face censorship, arrest, and—according to some reports—torture. Discrimination against ethnic minorities—especially the Kurds of northeastern Syria—is also a major source of concern. Observers in Syria and beyond continue to hope that al-Assad will follow through on his vow to protect human rights.

Find links to up-to-date government information, current news headlines, interesting facts, customs, and photographs from Syria at www.vgsbooks.com.

Government

Syria's constitution, adopted in 1973, establishes the nation as a socialist state in which the government controls the economy. Citizens who are eighteen years of age or older can vote to elect the president, who must be a Muslim and who is nominated by the Baath Party—the nation's official political organization. The president serves a seven-year term and has wide powers, including naming upper-level government officials and commanding the army.

The Syrian legislature's 250 members are elected to four-year terms and meet to debate government policy and to enact laws. A high judicial council, headed by the nation's president, appoints judges to Syria's courts. The top judicial level is the Court of Cassation, which hears final appeals that come from lower courts at the provincial and local levels. In cases involving family matters, Islamic religious courts interpret sharia (traditional Islamic law).

Syria is divided into fourteen provinces, each with a governor appointed by the federal government. Officials from the central government also join local councils to help with administration and to maintain strong ties between the provinces and the capital.

THE PEOPLE

Syria's population of approximately 18 million people is growing rapidly. At its estimated rate of increase of 2.4 percent, it is expected to double in approximately 29 years. An average Syrian woman has three or four children in her lifetime. Another indication of the nation's growth is the large proportion of young people, with about 40 percent of Syrians under the age of 15.

Syria's average population density is 251 people per square mile (97 per sq. km), compared to 1,121 people per square mile (433 people per sq. km) in neighboring Lebanon and 79 per square mile (30 per sq. km) in the United States. But the concentration of people in western Syria, especially in cities, is actually much higher, as the Syrian Desert and some of the most inaccessible mountainous areas are sparsely populated.

◉ Ethnic Groups

Syria is home to many different ethnic groups. However, the majority of Syrians—about 90 percent—are Arabs. Arabs share a common heritage

and language, but subgroups exist within this broad category. For example, the Bedouin make up a small percentage of Syria's Arabs.

The remaining 10 percent of Syrians belong to non-Arab ethnic groups—mainly to Kurdish, Armenian, and Turkoman communities. The Kurds are the country's largest non-Arab group, making up an estimated 8 to 9 percent of the Syrian population. They inhabit the northeastern corner of Syria, near Iraq and Turkey. The Syrian Kurds are only a small part of the Middle East's Kurdish population. Several million more Kurds inhabit the region where Syria, Turkey, Iraq, and Iran meet—an area often called Kurdistan.

Kurds in Syria and beyond have faced years of discrimination, restricted rights and, at times, violence from the majority population and the Arab-dominated government. These tensions have been aggravated by the war in Iraq, which also has a significant Kurdish minority. In March 2004, clashes erupted between Kurds, Arabs, and Syrian police. In the course of the unrest, which spread through several cities in northeastern Syria and lasted several days, at least twenty-five people were killed and hundreds were arrested. Furthermore, human rights reports by international agencies indicate that arrests of Kurds—often for no clear legal reason—are increasing and that the treatment of those arrested has become more harsh.

Other ethnic minorities in Syria include Armenians and Turkomans. The ancestors of Syria's Armenians fled Turkey in the early 1900s to escape Turkish oppression. Modern Syrian Armenians live mainly in and around Aleppo. They are Christian and continue to follow their own traditions and to run their own schools. Many Armenians work as traders or craftspeople.

Syria's small population of Turkomans originated in central Asia. Once a nomadic people, many members of the group still herd livestock in Al-Jazira and farm small plots near Aleppo. Most are Sunni Muslims who share religious beliefs with Syria's Arab Sunnis.

Most Syrians identify more strongly with their religious or ethnic community than with their shared nationality, and historical rivalry among some of Syria's various groups can complicate matters further. The result is a disunity among Syria's people, vividly illustrated by the situation of the Kurds. This problem is one of the nation's biggest and oldest challenges and has hampered national unity for decades.

These **Kurdish** women and children live in a rural area of northern Syria.

This **souk** in Damascus is located in ancient Roman buildings.

◉ Lifestyle

Many urban Syrians participate in both traditional and modern lifestyles. Most Syrian cities are centered in an old commercial and residential section, which may have been built before the Greek era. Traditional souks sell crafts, foods, and other goods. Beyond the old city, however, are modern buildings, including businesses and homes that use the up-to-date technology found in urban areas worldwide.

Most rural people, on the other hand, continue to follow primarily traditional customs that have changed little over Syria's history. The main livelihood is still farming, although more people own the land they work than farmers did in previous decades. Livestock herding is also a big part of rural Syrian life, and shepherds tend flocks in the mountains and plains. Improvements in transportation allow villagers to travel to cities for medical care, and their children may go to school in larger towns. Some young rural people also move to urban areas in search of jobs.

LIFE IN THE SYRIAN DESERT

The word *Bedouin* comes from the Arabic word *Badawi*, meaning "dweller of the desert." Traditional Bedouin live in large, woven tents. Each tent represents a family, and a group of families makes up a clan. Clan and family ties tend to be extremely strong, and loyalty and kinship is central to Bedouin life.

Living in the desert's difficult environment, the Bedouin have developed a tradition of hospitality. It is said that a traveler who comes to a Bedouin tent can never be refused food and shelter. The desert's demands have also formed a strong people, and Bedouin have a reputation among other Arabs for great courage.

Most Bedouin make their homes, at least for part of the year, in the desert. Members of this traditionally nomadic group herd camels and sheep through the Syrian Desert on a seasonal search for water and food. Syria's Bedouin share this lifestyle with other Middle Eastern Bedouin who migrate among Iraq, Saudi Arabia, Kuwait, and Jordan. However, some modern Bedouin have decided to follow a more settled lifestyle.

Syria's Kurds—despite the discrimination that they face—have been able to preserve many aspects of their distinct culture by living in relatively remote regions of the nation. A Sunni Islamic people, most Syrian Kurdish live a largely traditional lifestyle, inhabiting small villages and doing farmwork. Some have moved to larger towns and cities, where they usually work as manual laborers and where they often adopt Arabic dress.

Syrian women also have a changing role in their nation's life. The Syrian constitution outlaws discrimination based on gender. The Baath Party has long supported women's equality—in part, as a way to gain the approval of women voters. These measures have made improvements in women's status. In the 2000s, Syrian women make up approximately one-quarter to one-third of the nation's workforce. Women have also made major strides in political life, with a small but growing number of women elected to the nation's legislature.

Organizations such as the Syrian Women's Union, founded in 1967, work to gain improvements in Syrian women's education, employment, health, and other rights.

But Syrian women do still face discrimination. Religious and ethnic practices play a large part in determining the treatment of women. For example, some interpretations of Islam define guidelines for women's dress, behavior in public, and other customs. In addition, many rural women may find it harder to break out of traditional roles, in which women are charged primarily with the care of the children and the household.

To learn more about the people of Syria, go to www.vgsbooks.com and explore links to information about different ethnic groups, customs, and population statistics.

◓ Language

Nearly all Syrians speak Arabic, the nation's official language and the main tongue of the entire Arab world. Within Syria, a separate dialect (variation of the standard language) called Syrian Arabic is used in daily speech.

Syria's rich ethnic mixture also affects language patterns. Kurdish is related to Persian—the language used in Iran and other nearby nations. Kurdish is spoken among Kurds in the extreme northeastern corner of the country. However, teaching the language in public schools is banned. The publication of books and magazines in Kurdish is also officially illegal, but some materials are available.

The Armenian community uses Armenian at home. Similarly, Turkomans usually communicate in their native Turkic language, although most also use Arabic. In addition, because of French colonial influences in the twentieth century, many educated people in large cities speak French as a second language. Many university students study English as well.

> **Aramaic is the ancient language introduced to the region by the Aramaeans more than three thousand years ago. It is still spoken in three Syrian villages that are located in the mountains north of Damascus.**

Health

Syria's government provides health care to its citizens, usually at no cost to the patient. Although hospitals and medical workers tend to cluster in urban areas—especially in Damascus and Aleppo—clinics have opened throughout the country. Rural facilities sometimes do not have adequate equipment or staff.

Infectious diseases have long been one of Syria's biggest health problems. However, a national vaccination program has helped control some dangerous diseases, such as tuberculosis. Reported cases of the highly contagious disease diphtheria have also fallen dramatically over the past decade. But measles cases appear to be on the rise, even though vaccination against this illness has been largely successful. Trachoma (an eye disease) remains a problem, especially in rural areas.

One ongoing challenge to Syrian health care is the Palestinian population within the country. Thousands of Palestinians have settled in Syria, most in crowded temporary camps that offer substandard housing, inadequate health care, and limited resources. These living conditions lead to a higher incidence of disease in the camps, as well as higher rates of malnourishment and other health problems. With the help of international health organizations, Syria has attempted to address these issues, opening facilities such as the Husseinieh Health Center outside Damascus to provide care to Palestinians.

Yet despite such remaining difficulties, statistics show Syria's population overall to be increasingly healthy. The nation's infant mortality rate of 18 deaths in every 1,000 live births is relatively low for western Asia and is a dramatic improvement over rates from the early 1990s, which were twice as high. Syrian life expectancy, at an average of 70 years (71 for women and 69 for men), is typical for the region. And fortunately for Syrians, few cases of the deadly virus HIV (human immunodeficiency virus)/AIDS (acquired immunodeficiency syndrome) have been found in the country.

Education

Upon gaining independence in 1946, the Syrian government launched a concentrated effort to teach more of its citizens to read and write. More than half a century later, these efforts have been largely successful, and an estimated three-quarters of the adult population is literate.

All Syrian children are officially required to attend six years of primary school, beginning at the age of six, and most boys and girls do attend elementary classes. But fewer than half of these students continue on to the secondary level of schooling, which also lasts six years.

Some Syrian graduates go on to higher education at universities or technical-training institutes, and the total enrollment at these postsecondary schools is close to 200,000. The nation has four major universities, the primary one being the University of Damascus, founded in 1923. Universities are also located in Aleppo, Homs, and Latakia.

READING RATES

Although overall literacy is quite high in Syria, a wide gap exists between men and women. Approximately 88 percent of men are literate, while only an estimated 61 percent of Syrian women are able to read and write. This discrepancy may be partly due to the fact that fewer girls attend school than boys. This can be especially true in rural or traditional households, where girls are expected to become homemakers and are not encouraged to pursue education. Recent policies have begun to give women more rights. Several programs have been started specifically to address the problem of illiteracy among Syrian women.

CULTURAL LIFE

Syria's long history as a geographical and cultural gateway between the Mediterranean and the Middle East brought frequent takeovers and a great many invaders to the land over the years. But it has also left the nation with a wealth of influences that combine to create Syria's rich cultural life.

▶ Religion

Religious ties play a very important part in Syrian society. In fact, just as people tend to have strong ethnic alliances, most also feel a stronger loyalty to their religious group than to the nation.

About 85 percent of Syria's people follow the Islamic faith. Founded in the seventh century by the prophet Muhammad, Islam has two main sects—the Sunnis and the Shiites. They both support the central practices of the faith. In Syria, as in most of the Arab world, the Sunnis are the largest group, making up about 72 percent of the nation's Islamic population. Sunnis dominated political

activity for decades, until the al-Assad regime took power. The number of Shiites in Syria is small.

Both Sunni and Shiite Muslims are encouraged to fulfill certain religious duties. Believers pray to Allah (the Arabic word for God) five times daily, facing in the direction of Mecca, the Saudi Arabian city where Muhammad was born. They are called to prayer by muezzins (criers), who chant from minarets (towers). Every Muslim also tries to make the hajj, a pilgrimage to Mecca, at least once in his or her lifetime.

In addition to Sunnis and Shiites, the Islamic population in Syria includes three smaller sects. The nation's largest religious minority is the Alawis, who form about 10 percent of the Islamic group. Their beliefs include practices from Syria's Christian and Islamic periods. Alawis celebrate the Christian holidays of Easter and Christmas, for example, and also recognize traditional Islamic duties. Long persecuted for their religious ideas, the Alawis gained great power in 1971, when the Alawi general Hafez al-Assad became president.

Smaller in number than the Alawis are the Ismailis. Members of this group are closely related to Shiites and sometimes are called Seveners. The name comes from a split among Shiites that took place in about the ninth century. Until that time, all Shiites had accepted the same six imams (holy men with spiritual and earthly authority). A disagreement arose among Shiites about Ismail, the seventh imam of Islam. One group, the Ismailis, came to recognize no imams after Ismail. Most other Shiites supported a total of twelve imams, and members of this group are sometimes referred to as Twelvers.

The Druze in Syria make up about 2 to 3 percent of the religious population and live mostly in the southwestern district of Jabal al-Arab. They are a tightly knit and fiercely independent group. Originating as a branch of Shiite Islam in the eleventh century, the Druze derive their name from a mystic named Ismail ad-Darazi. Ad-Darazi was a follower of Al-Hakim, whom the Druze believe was an earthly presence of God. Many Druze practices are highly secretive, due to historical persecution that once forced the group into hiding.

Non-Islamic minority religions also exist in Syria. Christians account for about 10 percent of the Syrian religious population and belong to many sects. The largest Christian groups are Greek Orthodox, Armenian Orthodox, Syrian Orthodox, and Greek Catholic. Other Christians include Maronites, Nestorians, Chaldeans, Roman Catholics, and Protestants.

Druze people gather for a religious celebration.

HOLY LAND

One of the best examples of Syria's religious diversity is a single site in Damascus that has been the home of four different places of worship. The first was an Aramean temple to Hadad, the god of storms and fertility. This structure then became the Roman Temple of Jupiter. Byzantine rulers constructed a Christian church dedicated to Saint John on the same site. And in approximately A.D. 705, the Umayyads built the Great Mosque (*left*), which stands on the site in modern times and in which the residents of Damascus still worship.

◉ Holidays and Festivals

With its mix of religions, Syria's population celebrates a wide range of holidays and festivals. For Syria's large majority of Muslims, the Islamic holy month of Ramadan is one of the most important holiday seasons of the year. Ramadan commemorates Allah giving the Quran (Islam's holy text) to Muhammad, and the month is a time for fasting and prayer. Because Islamic holidays follow the lunar (moon-based) calendar, the date of Ramadan changes each year. Most adult Muslims neither eat nor drink from sunup to sundown during this month. After dark a meal called the *iftar* is eaten, and at the end of Ramadan, Syrian Muslims celebrate with the great feast of Eid al-Fitr. This holiday lasts for three or four days and gives everyone a chance to rejoice and to reflect on the past month. Gifts are often exchanged, and some cities hold festive street fairs with rides, fireworks, and other entertainment.

Eid al-Adha, or the Feast of the Sacrifice, is another major holiday. The festival falls during the hajj and celebrates the journey of the pilgrims. Eid al-Adha also recalls a story in the Quran in which a father who is willing to sacrifice his son for Allah is rewarded for his faith.

Syrian Christians celebrate Christmas to commemorate the birth of Jesus. During the Christmas season, many merchants at the souks sell decorations and special holiday sweets. Christmas Eve and Christmas Day are celebrated with church services, family dinners, bonfires, and songs. A few days later, at Epiphany, the Christmas camel brings gifts to good children. Easter is also an important holiday for Syria's Christian population.

Political holidays in Syria include Independence Day on April 17, commemorating the end of French rule, and Martyrs' Day on May 6, honoring Syrians who fought against the Ottomans in World War I. Syria's other secular (nonreligious) celebrations include Latakia's annual Mahabba Festival, an August event that draws huge crowds of tourists with sports competitions, art shows, and other cultural activities. Another popular attraction is the springtime Palmyra Desert Festival, which takes place near the ruins of this ancient city and showcases folk dancing performances, music, crafts, and horse and camel races.

Camels are prepared for competition at the racetrack in Palmyra.

Kibbeh, ground lamb with pine nuts, is a popular dish in Syria.

◉ Food

Syrian cuisine draws upon broad Middle Eastern cooking traditions, using common ingredients such as lamb, eggplant, rice, chickpeas, yogurt, bulgur (cracked wheat), and olive oil. Other meats, fresh vegetables, and seasonal or dried fruits occasionally supplement the usual foods. City dwellers tend to have a more varied diet than rural people do.

Traditional Syrian meals begin with meze, an appetizer course that often includes hummus, a finely blended mixture of chickpeas, lemon juice, garlic, and ground sesame seeds. This thick sauce is usually eaten with flat rounds of bread. Tabbouleh is another popular dish, combining bulgur with tomatoes, parsley, onions, oil, and lemon juice in a refreshing salad. Main courses are often made with lamb, and include popular dishes such as kibbeh (ground lamb mixed with bulgar and pine nuts and eaten either baked or raw) and *maqluba*, a rich entrée of lamb with eggplant, spices, and rice. *Mansaf*, a similar dish, is a traditional Bedouin meal of lamb and rice in a creamy yogurt sauce. Chicken is also commonly eaten, and seafood is popular along the coast, showing up in dishes such as *sayyadieh*, or "fisherman's meal"—a hearty stew of fish and rice.

Most Syrian dinners end with sweet Turkish coffee or strong tea served in small glasses. Fresh fruit is a common dessert choice, but for diners with more of a sweet tooth, pastries such as baklava or *kunafi*— rich with honey, spices, and nuts—hit the spot.

HUMMUS

Hummus is one of the simplest and most popular Syrian appetizers. Serve it with vegetables or wedges of fresh pita bread.

1 15-ounce can chickpeas

2 to 3 tablespoons store-bought tahini (sesame seed paste)

2 cloves garlic, peeled and crushed

juice of 2 lemons (about 6 tablespoons)

½ teaspoon salt

⅛ teaspoon cumin

parsley sprigs

1 teaspoon paprika

olive oil

1. Reserve the liquid from the canned chickpeas. Combine chickpeas, tahini, garlic, lemon juice, salt, and cumin in a blender or food processor. Add a little of the reserved chickpea liquid and process until mixture is a smooth paste. Add more liquid if the mixture is too dry or crumbly.
2. Place hummus in a wide, shallow serving dish. Garnish with parsley, and sprinkle with paprika and a few drops of olive oil.

Serves 4

Literature

Like other Middle Eastern countries, Syria takes great pride in its long tradition of oral and written poetry. Among the nation's most famous poets is Abu al-Ala al-Maarri, who was born in Maarrah, near Aleppo, in A.D. 973. Blinded by illness as a child, al-Maarri became a poet, teacher, and philosopher, whose beautiful and unique verse is still loved by modern readers.

The works of writers and scholars like al-Maarri developed alongside a tradition of oral legends. Storytellers entertained listeners with tales of ancient heroes and heroines. Many of these imaginative stories became the basis of *The Thousand and One Nights,* a collection of age-old folktales from the Arab world that was compiled in the 1500s.

Some of the major authors to emerge in the years following independence included the poets Nizar Qabbani and Ali Ahmad Said (who uses the name Adonis), and the poet and playwright Mohammed al-Maghout. Many postindependence writings reflected the struggles that Syria faced in the wake of French control. Some authors tackled the subject of the Arab world's conflict with Israel. Halim Barakat, who was born in Syria and has since lived in Lebanon and the United

States, addressed this issue in his 1961 novel *Six Days*. Barakat has also written many other books, essays, articles, and nonfiction books and has worked as a sociology professor.

Once Hafez al-Assad came to power in 1970, his regime banned the works of some authors who criticized the government too openly or too harshly. As a result, these writers were forced to publish their books outside Syria, mainly in Lebanon. So far, Bashar al-Assad has continued to limit freedom of speech. Nevertheless, some authors such as Ulfat Idilbi do continue to write in Syria. Idilbi has written many short stories, as well as two novels. Her works describe life in modern Syria.

◉ Music and Dance

Listening to poetry read aloud is one of the most traditional listening pleasures in Syria, and it remains a popular form of entertainment. Syrian musicians often accompany readers, usually playing traditional instruments such as the oud (an Arabian lute), the rebab (a fiddle), and the kanoon (a many-stringed instrument). These stringed instruments are often backed by drums or jingling percussion in rhythm with the music.

Musicians also play Syrian folk music at local and regional celebrations. Such celebrations frequently feature folk dancing as well. The Inana dance group stages shows of classic Syrian dance at home and beyond. In addition, ethnic minorities preserve their heritage through dance. For example, the Kurdish community still performs its own traditional dances, most of which follow a form known as *govand*. A group of dancers hold hands in a circle while performing the dance's footwork, usually surrounding one or two dancers in the center of the circle.

Modern music also has many fans in Syria, and a number of pop stars play to large audiences. The most famous of all is George Wassouf, whose distinctive voice and catchy songs have made him

WORDS FROM ANCIENT SYRIA

LXVIII
There is a palace,
and the ruined wall
Divides the sand,
a very home of tears,
And where love whispered of
a thousand years
The silken-footed caterpillars
crawl.

LXXXII
The rolling, ever-rolling years
of time
Are as a diwan
of Arabian song;
The poet, headstrong and
supremely strong,
Refuses to repeat a single
rhyme.

—from the *Diwan* of
Abu al-Ala al-Maarri

Ruwaida Attieh appeared on the Arabic television show *Super Star* in 2003.

SYRIA'S NEXT BIG STAR?

Many young Syrians enjoy watching new musical talent on *Super Star*. This Arabic-language version of the *American Idol* television show pits contestants from different Middle Eastern countries against one another. The program is very popular, but regional hostilities often come into play when it's time to vote. For example, depending on relations between the countries, viewers in Syria might refuse to vote for any Lebanese contestant and vice versa.

hugely popular in Syria and the rest of the Middle East. Another Syrian star is Mayada Al Hinawi, a female vocalist who has been recording albums for more than two decades. Ruwaida Attieh is newer on the scene, but she is widely regarded as a rising star and is also embarking on an acting career.

◉ Visual Arts

As a crossroads of trade, Syria has welcomed artists and artistic forms from Africa, Asia, and Europe. Many traditional Syrian crafts reflect these varied influences.

Since the Middle Ages (A.D. 500–1500), Damascus has been famous for making silk and steel, and these two materials are the basis for two traditional Syrian arts. Damask cloth—named after Damascus—is a treasured handicraft. This rich fabric, made of silk, wool, cotton, linen, or other textiles, bears intricate patterns created by the weaving process. A similar product is fine, handmade brocade—silk cloth richly interwoven with silver and gold threads. These beautiful fabrics continue to be made in Syria.

Steel is the basic material for traditional damascene, named after Damascus. The earliest damascene makers used a special technique to forge the steel into swords and knives decorated with a fine wavy pattern. These weapons were famous for their exceptional strength, flexibility, and beauty. This technique for making damascene has largely been lost over time. However, a modern relative is used to inlay decorative patterns of gold or silver into plaques, trays, and other goods. This kind of damascene is especially popular in the form of jewelry. Woodworking, glassblowing, and pottery are other Syrian crafts with long traditions.

Because the Quran forbids the use of human figures in Islamic decoration, much of Syria's visual art has traditionally focused on geometric and floral patterns. Pages from the Quran are decorated with elaborate designs, along with fine calligraphy (hand-lettering). In addition, mosaic tiling decorates mosques with a variety of beautiful patterns and styles, and intricately inlaid wooden furniture is widely found.

In addition to Syria's many traditional crafts, modern artists add to the country's rich artistic heritage. Many study art in Europe or the United States and then return to Syria, and many combine Western artistic techniques and ideas with traditional Syrian themes. However, Syrian art is wide ranging in its subjects and forms. Painters include Thaier Helal, whose pattern-oriented works recall the intricate designs of Islamic art, while Safwan Dahoul's paintings—all of which are named "Réve" (the French word for "dream")—usually depict women. Malva Omar Hamdi's paintings of landscapes and nature are

An artisan in Damascus creates geometric designs in his tile work.

displayed in museums around the world, and Sara Shamma's self-portraits have been shown in international competitions.

And painting is just one area in which Syrian artists work. Sculptor Mustafa Ali shapes subjects such as animals, human forms, and trees out of bronze and other materials. Other artists work with plastics, video, calligraphy, or other media. Galleries in Damascus and Aleppo showcase work by contemporary Syrian artists.

> If you would like to learn more about Syrian culture, visit www.vgsbooks.com, where you'll find links to recipes, poetry, photographs, and more.

Sports and Recreation

Soccer, called football in Syria, is one of the nation's top sports. Basketball, tennis, boxing, and swimming are also popular. In addition to male athletes, Syrian women are also becoming more involved in sports. Islamic traditions of modest dress—which require that women cover most of their bodies when in public—have historically restricted women from participating in sports. However, increased women's rights have given female athletes the chance to take part in national and international competitions in track and field and other sports. For example, in 1996 Ghada Shouaa became the first Syrian to win an Olympic gold medal when she won the hep-tathlon (a seven-part track-and-field event).

Syrians, especially in urban areas, also enjoy a variety of other recreational activities. In Damascus some Syrians enjoy European-style nightclubs and discotheques, while *qahwas*, or

Ghada Shouaa celebrates her win at the end of the heptathlon in July 1996.

coffeehouses, are more traditional destinations. Most qahwa customers are men, who gather to drink coffee or tea, to chat, and to play games such as dominoes and backgammon. Movie theaters scattered throughout city neighborhoods show both Syrian-made and foreign-made films. Usama Muhammad is one of Syria's most prominent directors. His films—such as *Sunduq al-Dunya* (called Box of Life or Sacrifices in English) and *Nujum al-Nahar* (Stars in Mid-Day)—have received praise at home and abroad.

Live theater also draws audiences, while for those who prefer to stay in, a number of television series are popular. Social comedies and family dramas are the most successful, especially those that use humor to examine the ups and downs of everyday Syrian life.

THE ECONOMY

In the turbulent Middle East, Syria's economy has always been subject to ups and downs depending on regional conflicts, global affairs, and its own internal strife. When the Baath Party took control of the Syrian government in 1971, it directed the nation's economy according to socialist policies such as shared landownership and state control of industries. But the nation's finances spiraled downward during the mid-1980s. Oil profits, which provided the majority of Syria's earned foreign income, fell as world petroleum prices decreased. To help the struggling nation get by, some of its Arab neighbors provided financial aid. But Syria's regionally unpopular decision to back Iran in its war against Iraq led to a drop in this aid.

To make up for declining income, the Syrian government cut some expenses and reduced imports. However, with ongoing concerns regarding Israel and Lebanon, the regime spent approximately half of its budget on defense.

In the late 1980s and early 1990s, these factors placed Syria's economy in an uncertain position. After the 1991 Persian Gulf War—in which Syria had been on the popluar side, against Iraq— other Arab countries began offering Syria increased aid to help the nation get back on track. Oil production rose, although fluctuating world oil prices affected Syria's income from petroleum. Agricultural crop yields also improved, but severe droughts in 1997 and 1999 took a heavy toll on farmers and herders.

When Bashar al-Assad took office in 2000, he pledged to introduce reforms, to loosen government control over the economy, and to allow greater modernization. Yet, he and his government have been slow to introduce significant changes. Then, with the outbreak of the 2003 Iraq conflict and the placement of U.S. sanctions against Syria in 2004, the nation's economic footing began to slip once again. Syrians and international observers alike hope that the nation will soon find the means to pull out of its slump.

The Petroleum Industry

Like many other nations in the Middle East, Syria gets much of its income from oil. It first awarded rights for oil exploration to a foreign firm in the 1930s, and outside businesses dominated the nation's petroleum industry until the 1960s. Following the transfer from private to state control in 1964, however, the oil sector emerged as a major national money earner. The main oil fields lie at Qaratshuk, Suwaidi, and Rumaylah in northeastern Syria. To further involve itself in the oil industry, in 1976 Syria joined the Organization of Petroleum Exporting Countries (OPEC), a group that sets quotas and prices for oil in world markets.

Syrian oil production peaked in 1995, with an output of about 600,000 barrels a day. But output has slowed significantly since then, and some experts estimate that the nation has no more than ten years' worth of petroleum reserves left. With a rapidly growing population, Syria may soon have to import oil to fill its energy needs.

Syria's oil reserves are small compared to those of other Arab states in the region. The nation is estimated to pump about 535,000 barrels of petroleum per day, compared to the millions of barrels a day produced in Saudi Arabia. Nevertheless, oil sales account for about half of the country's overall export income and are its chief source of foreign revenue.

Along with crude oil exports, Syria has sometimes been able to earn some income from transit fees for oil pipelines. In addition to the internal pipelines that carry crude oil between Syria's fields and refineries, a number of pipelines enter Syria from other nations and cross the country to reach refineries and Mediterranean ports. Outside nations pay Syria a fee to use these channels, but regional unrest prevents this source of revenue from being stable. For example, a pipeline once brought crude oil from Kirkuk, Iraq, to a refinery at Homs and from there to the Syrian port of Baniyas. However, the outbreak of war between Iran and Iraq caused Syria to close the Kirkuk-Baniyas pipeline in 1982. It was reported to be in use again in 2000 or 2001 but was shut down once more after the outbreak of the Iraq conflict in March 2003.

In more positive developments, Syria awarded new oil exploration rights to foreign companies in 2003 and 2004. In July 2004, Syria and China announced plans to cooperate in developing a new oil field in the northeastern part of the country.

Workers harvest **wheat.** Agriculture makes up one-quarter of Syria's economy.

Agriculture

Agriculture was once the cornerstone of the Syrian economy. It has dropped to second place behind oil as a foreign-income earner. But it is still a major factor in the nation's life and finances. Agriculture makes up about one-quarter of Syria's gross domestic product (GDP, the total annual value of goods and services produced within the country's borders) and employs approximately one-third of the nation's workers. While the government still maintains considerable authority, national control over agriculture began to lessen during the 1990s.

The greatest obstacle facing Syrian farmers is a lack of water. Rainfall along the coast is sufficient

RUNNING DRY

Water shortages have long been one of Syria's most persistent problems. Severe droughts in the late 1990s led to strict controls on water usage, and the water supply remains a major concern. While city dwellers find water outages an inconvenience, drought is especially hard on nomadic Bedouin herders. As scrub vegetation and grazing land for goats and sheep dries up and dies, some Bedouin bring their herds westward to farming areas.

for farming, but irrigation is essential for crops planted farther inland. The Euphrates and Orontes rivers provide most of the water for this irrigation. The Euphrates Dam, built in the 1970s, was intended to double the amount of cropland with its large reservoir. However, high costs and low water levels have slowed down the predicted expansion of arable land.

In all, about 25 percent of Syria's land is farmed, primarily along the coast and in the north. Although mechanization (the use of machinery) is becoming more common, many farmers still use traditional manual methods. Cereal grains, sugar beets, cotton, and fruits and vegetables are Syria's principal crops. The chief cereals are wheat, barley, and corn. An age-old crop, cotton was once Syria's biggest export. In modern times, the nation's textile mills use most of the cotton, but about 20 percent is still exported. Among orchard crops, olives are of first importance, and in the Aleppo area, pistachio nuts are grown. On the coastal plain and in northwestern Syria, farmers harvest grapes, which supply a small wine industry. Other fruit crops include figs, melons, cherries, and apricots.

Sheep, poultry, and goats are the leading livestock animals, and herds of both beef and dairy cattle have also increased. Syria produces substantial amounts of meat, eggs, and milk products.

Syria does not have a major fishing industry, although small crews do pull in catches of tuna, sardines, and other fish and seafood. Hoping to create a more reliable source of food, the government is working to establish fish farms along the coast and inland to raise specific breeds of fish.

Mining, Manufacturing, and Energy

In the 1940s, geologists discovered natural gas in northeastern Syria while searching for petroleum deposits. The government allowed foreign firms to develop this resource, and groups from France, Czechoslovakia, and the United States built processing centers. The main refinery is at Homs, and another plant is under construction at Rumaylah.

A man tends a flock of sheep near Homs. A **fertilizer factory** is visible in the background.

Syria also contains large deposits of phosphate (a rock used to make fertilizer and other chemical products), which workers have extracted since the 1970s. The largest mine, located in central Syria, produces about 2.3 million tons (2.1 million metric tons) of phosphate per year. Most goes to European countries, while Syrian farmers also use some as fertilizer. Smaller reserves of natural asphalt, salt, and iron also exist.

Much of Syria's industrial sector is dedicated to processing mined phosphate, iron, and asphalt. Factories also process agricultural goods, doing work such as pressing olives into oil or refining sugar from sugar beets. Other plants turn out commercial goods such as glass, paper, and household appliances.

Syria's textile industry is a key part of the nation's manufacturing sector. Locally grown cotton is spun into thread at factories in Aleppo, Hama, and Damascus. Workers weave cotton, wool, and other fabrics using modern techniques. And while the production of damask and silk brocade has been mechanized to some degree, these long valued exports are still sometimes made by hand. Altogether, manufacturing and industry are responsible for about one-quarter of the nation's GDP.

In October 2004, the Iranian car manufacturer Saipa opened a jointly owned Iranian-Syrian factory near Damascus. Although Iran controls most of the company, this type of financial cooperation could be a way to help Syria's economy get back on its feet. As an added bonus, Saipa's Pride car uses little fuel and has been proposed as an ideal model for taxi drivers in Damascus and other big cities.

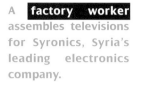

A **factory worker** assembles televisions for Syronics, Syria's leading electronics company.

Syria's industrial sector is its largest user of energy. At one time, hydropower from the Euphrates and other dams filled Syria's energy needs. However, these dams have been unable to meet increasing energy demands, and Syria has turned to alternate sources. Among these replacements are solar power (using the sun's energy) and nuclear reactors.

Even the use of these other sources has not prevented power outages in Syrian cities that can last up to four hours per day. Because many industries have had to decrease production to accommodate frequent power shortages, Syria's energy crunch has seriously affected manufacturing.

Transportation

As a major crossroads of trade, Syria has long had transportation networks for moving goods to international markets. These systems have historically been centered in western Syria. After independence, the government worked to extend roads and railways throughout the country. Very few people in modern Syria own cars, and personal travel is usually accomplished by bus, by train, or on foot.

Most of Syria's highways and major roads are in the west and cover more than 15,500 miles (24,944 km) of the country's territory. They run between Damascus and other large cities and carry most of the nation's freight and passengers. Two-lane roads connect towns and small settlements.

Syria has two railway systems, both originally built in the early 1900s. One track was part of the Hejaz Railway that connected Damascus and Dara in Syria with cities in Lebanon and Jordan. This railway covers about 203 miles (327 km), while another set of tracks extends for more than 1,400 miles (2,253 km). Rail connections are available for freight and passengers between major urban areas in western Syria. Tracks also cross the width of the nation, linking Aleppo, Al-Raqqah, Dayr az-Zawr, Al-Hasakah, and Al-Qamishli. All of Syria's railroads are owned by the national government.

The Syrian government also operates the national airline, Syrian Arab Airlines. The airline provides flights to many points in Asia, Europe, and Africa and maintains an international airport at Damascus. Smaller airfields exist at Aleppo, Latakia, and Dayr az-Zawr. Syria's chief seaports are at Latakia, Tartus, and Baniyas.

Trade, Tourism, and Services

Syria's principal trade exports are oil, fruits and vegetables, textiles, and raw cotton. Italy is the destination for most of these goods, followed by France, Turkey, Saudi Arabia, and Spain. Imports consist mainly of foodstuffs, machinery, vehicles, and other manufactured goods. Germany is the largest single source of these products, with other major suppliers being France, Italy, and Turkey.

Tourism is another important area of Syria's economy. The terrorist attacks of September 11, 2001, the U.S. war in Iraq, and the uncertain political situation in the Middle East have discouraged many American and European tourists from traveling

HAPPY TO BE HERE

Despite various challenges, Syria's tourism industry continues to draw visitors to the nation. Ancient Roman ruins, stone forts from the era of the Crusades, and stately mosques all draw history buffs. The bustling souks of Damascus and Aleppo also have much to offer shoppers. Newer attractions include the Happy Land Amusement Park, which opened outside of Damascus in 1998. Built with help and funds from Saudi Arabia, the park features rides, a swimming pool, video arcades, and more.

This very well-preserved **Roman theater** in Busra dates from the second century A.D. and is one of the many ancient sites that attracts tourists to Syria. To learn more about the tourist attractions of Syria, visit www.vgsbooks.com.

to the area. Nevertheless, more than two million visitors do arrive annually (most of them from Lebanon, Jordan, and other Arab nations) to view Syria's ancient sites and to enjoy its natural scenery. These tourists boost Syria's foreign income by more than $1 billion. To accommodate these travelers and to attract even more, the nation has worked to improve access to its historic ruins and other archaeological treasures. In addition, many new tourism facilities were in progress or planned in the early 2000s. Many of Syria's service workers, who make up close to one-third of the nation's total workforce, hold jobs in the hotels, restaurants, shops, and other businesses that cater to tourists.

Visit vgsbooks.com for up-to-date information about Syria's economy and a converter with the current exchange rate where you can learn how many Syrian pounds are in one U.S. dollar.

◉ The Future

Once the proud gateway between the Mediterranean and the Middle East—two of the world's most important ancient regions—modern Syria has confronted a complex and daunting mix of drought, costly spending, fluctuating oil prices, and war. As these problems worsen, Syria has found it necessary to accept international aid. This aid, combined with the fact that Syria spends more money on imports than it earns from the sale of its exports, left the nation owing more than $20 billion to foreign lenders by the early 2000s. When the United States imposed sanctions against Syria in 2004, the country's heavy debt only became more overwhelming.

Meanwhile, unresolved issues with Israel and Lebanon loom, and the ongoing conflict in Iraq has added still more tension and violence to the region. All of these factors weigh on Syria's leaders and its citizens as they consider what the coming years have in store. Syria has long seen its fortunes rise and fall with the tides of global politics and local affairs. But as its people look ahead, they hope that their nation will finally be able to achieve a brighter future.

Timeline

5000 B.C.	Early livestock herders inhabit Greater Syria.
2500	The settlement of Ebla flourishes.
1800	The Phoenician civilization thrives.
333	Seleucus—a general of Alexander the Great—takes control of Syria.
64	Syria becomes part of the Roman Empire.
A.D. 273	Roman armies destroy Palmyra.
629	Early followers of Islam leave Mecca to spread the religion.
661	Muawiyah, a member of the Umayyad dynasty, is elected as caliph of the Islamic Empire.
715	The Abbasids overthrow the Umayyads.
973	The poet Abu al-Ala al-Maarri is born.
1096	The Crusades begin.
1174	Saladin becomes sultan of Egypt and Syria.
1260	Mongols invade Syria.
1402	Timur the Lame conquers Damascus.
1516	The Ottoman Turks take control of Syria.
1860	Fighting breaks out between the Druze and the Maronites.
LATE 1800s	Movements for Arab independence begin.
1914	World War I begins.
1916	France and Britain secretly sign the Sykes-Picot Agreement.
1918	Arab troops take Damascus. The Ottomans are defeated.
1920	The French mandate over Syria takes effect.
1923	Damascus University is founded.
1925	Syrians rebel against French rule.
1939	World War II breaks out.
1941	The Germans take over the Syrian government from France. Charles de Gaulle promises Syria eventual independence.
1945	The Germans are defeated. Syrians revolt against French control.

1946   French troops leave Syria, and the nation is independent.

1948   The State of Israel is created. The Arab-Israeli conflict is won by Israel.

MID-1950s   The Baath Party begins to gain strength.

1958   Syria and Egypt form the United Arab Republic (UAR).

1961   The UAR dissolves. Halim Barakat's novel *Six Days* is published.

1967   The Six-Day War takes place. Syria loses the Golan Heights to Israel.

1970   Troops under the command of General Hafez al-Assad surround a Baath Party meeting. Al-Assad becomes the party's leader.

1971   Al-Assad becomes president of Syria.

1973   A third Arab-Israeli conflict is fought.

1976   Syria sends troops into Lebanon during that nation's civil war.

1980   The Iran-Iraq War begins. Syria sides with Iran, a widely unpopular move.

1982   Unrest in Hama ends in a government attack, leaving tens of thousands dead and injured.

1984   Syrian athlete Joseph Atiyeh wins a silver medal in wrestling at the Summer Olympics in Los Angeles, California.

1991   Following Iraq's 1990 invasion of Kuwait, the Persian Gulf War begins.

1996   Ghada Shouaa wins a gold medal in the heptathlon at the Summer Olympics in Atlanta, Georgia.

1997   Severe drought strikes Syria.

2000   Hafez al-Assad dies. His son Bashar al-Assad takes power.

2003   A U.S.-led war against Iraq begins. Israel bombs a suspected Palestinian terrorist site near Damascus.

2004   The United States places economic sanctions on Syria for its suspected involvement in terrorism. Syrian troops in Lebanon are reorganized but not withdrawn.

COUNTRY NAME Syrian Arab Republic

AREA 71,498 square miles (185,180 sq. km)

MAIN LANDFORMS Anti-Lebanon Mountains, Coastal Plain, Jabal al-Nusayriyah, Great Rift Valley, Syrian Plateau, Syrian Desert

HIGHEST POINT Mount Hermon, 9,232 feet (2,814 m) above sea level

LOWEST POINT Unnamed location near Lake Tiberias, 656 feet (200 m) below sea level. (Also known as the Sea of Galilee, Lake Tiberias lies in the disputed terriotry of the Golan Heights.)

MAJOR RIVERS Euphrates, Orontes, Barada

ANIMALS Deer, gazelles, dormice, hares, hedgehogs, weasels, foxes, chameleons

CAPITAL CITY Damascus

OTHER MAJOR CITIES Aleppo, Hama, Homs, Latakia

OFFICIAL LANGUAGE Arabic

MONETARY UNIT Syrian pound. 1 pound = 100 piastres.

SYRIAN CURRENCY

The Syrian pound—also called the lira—became the official Syrian currency in 1920, replacing the Ottoman lira. Under French rule, the pound was also used in Lebanon between 1924 and 1948 and was issued by the French-controlled Banque de Syrie et du Liban (Bank of Syria and Lebanon). In 1956 a new, Syrian-owned Central Bank opened, and it remains the only legal issuer of the national currency. Syrian bills come in denominations of 1, 5, 10, 25, 50, 100, 200, 500, and 1,000 pounds. Coins are also minted in values of 1, 5, 10, and 25 pounds. The smaller denomination of piastres is rarely used anymore. Syrian history, architecture, culture, and economy are represented on the country's currency, with scenes depicting Saladin, the ruins of Palmyra, the Euphrates Dam, farming and industrial work, the waterwheels of Hama, and many other designs.

Syria's flag is composed of three wide, horizontal stripes. From the top, they are solid red, white with two green stars, and solid black. This flag, which was also that of the short-lived United Arab Republic (1958–1961), was adopted by Syria in 1980. During the UAR, the stars represented Syria and Egypt and they may still, although some observers say that they stand for Syria and Iraq. The meaning of the bands of color is also debated. One theory states that the red represents Syria's long struggle and sacrifice for freedom, the white stands for peace, and the black recalls the dark years of foreign rule. Another interpretation says that the red is symbolic of blood shed by Syrian heroes, while the white, green, and black all symbolize different historical dynasties.

Syria's national anthem is titled "Homat el Diyar" ("Guardians of the Homeland"). It was adopted in 1936, when the nation was still under French control. The anthem's words were written by Khalil Mardam Bey, with music composed by Mohammad Salim Flayfel and Ahmad Salim Flayfel. An English translation of the first verse follows below.

Homat el Diyar (Guardians of the Homeland)

Defenders of the realm,
Peace on you;
Our proud spirits will
Not be subdued.
The adobe of Arabism,
A hallowed sanctuary;
The seat of the stars,
An inviolable preserve.

For a link to a site where you can listen to Syria's national anthem, go to www.vgsbooks.com.

Flag

National Anthem

BASHAR AL-ASSAD (b. 1965) Al-Assad was born near Latakia as the second son of former Syrian president Hafez al-Assad. Because his older brother, Basil, had been chosen by their father to follow in his footsteps, Bashar did not pursue politics. Instead, he studied medicine in Great Britain. But in 1994, Basil was killed in a car accident. Bashar suddenly became the likely candidate to succeed his father, and when Hafez al-Assad died in 2000, thirty-four-year-old Bashar took power. He pledged to modernize Syria and to introduce many reforms, but so far the pace of change has been gradual.

ULFAT IDILBI (b. 1912) Born in Damascus, Idilbi was married at the age of seventeen. Although she was never able to finish her schooling, she began writing in her thirties and soon won praise—as well as several awards—for her work. She has published many short stories, along with two novels. Her first novel, *Sabriya: Damascus Bitter Sweet*, was made into a Syrian television program.

USAMA MUHAMMAD (b. 1954) Usama Muhammad, born in Latakia, is one of Syria's best-known filmmakers. He studied film direction at Moscow University in Russia and returned to Syria to begin his career. He has both written and directed films, and in 1988 his first film, *Nujum al-Nahar (Stars in Mid-Day)*, was shown at the Cannes Film Festival in France. Although it went on to win international praise and prizes, government censorship has made it difficult for this movie—or any of Muhammad's films—to be shown within Syria.

NUREDDIN (1118–1174) Born in Damascus to the powerful atabeg (regional leader) Zangi, Nureddin grew up to be a skilled military commander and a unifying leader. At the age of twenty-eight, he succeeded his father as atabeg of Aleppo, while his brother took over in Mosul (in present-day Iraq). Nureddin soon began battling against the Christian armies who arrived in the region during the Crusades. His forces reclaimed significant amounts of Syrian territory, including Antioch. After they seized Damascus from the crusaders in 1154, much of Greater Syria was under the control of the Zangid dynasty, led by Nureddin and his brother.

SARA SHAMMA (b. 1975) Born in Damascus, Shamma completed studies at the city's Adham Ismail Fine Arts Institute at the age of twenty. She went on to earn a degree in fine arts from Damascus University, and after graduation she became an instructor at Adham Ismail. Shamma's paintings have been shown around the world, and she has won many awards, including fourth place in the 2004 BP Portrait Awards, held by the National Portrait Gallery in London, England.

GHADA SHOUAA (b. 1972) Born in Maharda, a town in central Syria, Shouaa is one of Syria's first prominent female athletes. Always athletic, she began training at the age of fourteen to compete in the heptathlon. She entered international competitions in the early 1990s, including the 1992 Summer Olympics in Barcelona, Spain. In her second Olympics, the 1996 Summer Games in Atlanta, Georgia, Shouaa won the gold medal in the women's heptathlon. Her victory marked Syria's first Olympic gold medal in history and only the third gold ever won by an Arab woman. Although Shouaa retired in 2000 after a series of injuries, she is still regarded as a hero in women's sports at home and around the world.

GEORGE WASSOUF (b. 1961) Born in the village of Kafroun, Wassouf loved singing as a boy and began performing at weddings and parties as a teenager. At the age of sixteen, he moved to Lebanon and soon began recording music. He remains a major star in Syria and throughout the Arab world. Known as the "Sultan of Tarab" (*tarab* is usually translated as "entertainment" or "amusement"), he has made more than twenty albums and has an enormous audience of fans.

ZENOBIA (ca. 241–?) Zenobia was the wife of Odenathus, a military commander and ruler of Palmyra. Following his death in 267, Zenobia became Palmyra's queen. Declaring the kingdom independent of Rome, she crowned her young son emperor. These bold acts got Rome's attention, and by 273 the Romans had destroyed the city and had taken Zenobia prisoner. Despite her defeat, she was renowned for both her courage and her beauty and is remembered as a noble warrior queen. Historian Philip K. Hitti describes her in his *History of Syria,* saying, "With pearly teeth and large flashing eyes, she conducted herself in regal dignity and pomp. . . . On state occasions she wore a purple robe fringed with gems and clasped with a buckle at the waist leaving one of her arms bare to the shoulder. She rode, helmet on head, in a carriage shining with precious stones."

BEEHIVE HOUSES Syria's cone-shaped "beehive houses" are some of the country's most unique structures. Made from mud and often painted white, most lie in north central Syria. Warm in the winter and cool during Syria's hot summers, they were originally built to withstand Syria's climate. Most beehive houses are used for storage, but families in some villages still live in the traditional dwellings.

CASTLES FROM THE CRUSADES During the Crusades (1096–1270), many forts and castles were built in Syria by both the Christian and Islamic armies. These imposing stone structures still stand in the western part of the country. Some of the most impressive are Aleppo's citadel, the Krak des Chevaliers near Homs, the castle at Masyaf, and the Qalaat Marqab near the Mediterranean coast south of Baniyas.

THE DEAD CITIES In the region surrounding Aleppo lie hundreds of abandoned cities from the Byzantine era (A.D. 400s and 500s). Built by Christian settlers and abandoned for unknown reasons, these ghost towns are filled with beautiful and mysterious ruins and are scattered throughout a striking hilly landscape. More than 750 of these cities have been found, and many have not yet been fully excavated. Some of the best-known are Qalb Lozeh, Al-Bara, and Qalaat Semaan.

NATIONAL MUSEUM This Damascus museum contains a wealth of artifacts illustrating Syrian history, from fourteenth-century B.C. clay tablets, all the way up to the room of an eighteenth-century palace. Other highlights include Phoenician pottery, a Roman sarcophagus (coffin), a reconstructed synagogue, and a gallery of breathtaking Islamic glasswork and ceramics.

OLD CITY OF DAMASCUS The old section of Syria's capital city has sights and activities for every visitor. The ancient Roman Arch and Saladin's tomb are treats for any history buff, and the spectacular Azem Palace, dating from the 1800s, is a stunning example of classic Damascene architecture. The Old City's Christian quarter holds a number of churches. In the larger Islamic section is the beautiful Great Mosque, or Umayyad Mosque, which is regarded by Muslims as one of the holiest sites in Islam. Shoppers can spend hours exploring the area's souks, markets specializing in everything from spices to bridal wear, and restaurants and cafés serve local dishes to hungry sightseers.

PALMYRA After the Romans destroyed Palmyra in A.D. 273, the once-great city never reclaimed its former glory. Ancient Palmyra is a labyrinth of reddish limestone ruins set against a dramatic desert landscape. The site, covering an area of more than 2 square miles (5 sq. km), contains remains of temples, tombs, government buildings, baths, and dozens of columns. One of the most impressive and well-preserved buildings is the Sanctuary of Bel, a large temple complex.

Baath Party: a socialist political party that supported socialism and pan-Arabism. Baathists took power in Syria and Iraq in the 1960s.

Crusades: a series of invasions and wars that took place between 1096 and 1270 in the Middle East. The crusaders' goal was to capture the Holy Land from the Muslims and claim Jerusalem for Christianity.

Holy Land: a name for the region comprised of modern-day Israel, the Palestinian territories, and surrounding lands, which were once part of Greater Syria. This area is very important to the three word religions of Judaism, Christianity, and Islam.

intifada: a broad Palestinian uprising against Israel, mostly carried out by Palestinian civilians rather than by terrorist factions. The first intifada began in 1987. The second, also known as the al-Aqsa Intifada, began in 2000.

Islam: a religion founded on the Arabian Peninsula in the seventh century A.D. by the prophet Muhammad. The religion's primary tenets are known as the Five Pillars of Islam. Most followers of Islam, called Muslims, are members of the Sunni sect, while others follow the Shiite branch of the religion. Most Syrians are Muslims.

pan-Arabism: a political movement that arose in the Middle East in the early 1900s. The goal of pan-Arabism was to form a united Arab state in the region.

Quran: the holy book of Islam. According to Islamic belief, the Quran's teachings were communicated by Allah (God) to the prophet Muhammad. These divine messages were later collected and recorded in a single volume, which was written in Arabic.

socialism: a political and economic theory based on the idea of social (shared) rather than individual ownership of goods

terrorism: acts of violence—often against civilians—committed by groups who are trying to force a government or other group of people to do what they want

United Nations: an international organization formed at the end of World War II in 1945 to help handle global disputes. The United Nations replaced a similar, earlier group known as the League of Nations.

Western: a geographic and political term that usually refers to the politics, culture, and history of the United States and Europe

Glossary

Cable News Network. *CNN.com International—Asia News*. 2004. http://edition.cnn.com/ASIA/ (December 13, 2004).
This site provides current events and breaking news about Syria, as well as a searchable archive of older articles.

Day, Alan J. "Syria: Economy." *Regional Surveys of the World: The Middle East and North Africa*. London: Europa Publications, 2003.
This article examines Syria's recent economic situation.

Europa World Yearbook, 2003. Vol. 2. London: Europa Publications, 2003.
Covering Syria's recent history, economy, and government, this annual publication also provides a wealth of statistics on population, employment, trade, and more.

Hitti, Philip K. *Syria: A Short History; Being a Condensation of the Author's History of Syria including Lebanon and Palestine*. New York: The Macmillan Company, 1959.
This classic volume by a renowned scholar describes Syrian history up to the mid-twentieth century in vivid, engaging detail.

Joris, Lieve. *The Gates of Damascus*. Oakland: Lonely Planet Publications, 1996.
This travel narrative offers a unique look at Syria from a woman's perspective, describing the experiences of a European visitor and her Syrian friend.

Lawrence, T. E. *Seven Pillars of Wisdom: A Triumph*. New York: Anchor Books, 1991.
Lawrence of Arabia's memoir offers readers a smart and colorful look at Syria at the time of World War I.

Lunn, Jon, ed. "Syria: History." *Regional Surveys of the World: The Middle East and North Africa*. London: Europa Publications, 2003.
This article surveys the events of recent Syrian history.

Al-Maarri, Abu al-Ala. *The Diwan of Abu'l-Ala*. London: J. Murray, 1948.
This volume of poems is by the prominent Syrian poet Abu al-Ala al-Maarri.

Mallowan, Agatha Christie. *Come, Tell Me How You Live*. New York: Dodd, Mead, & Co., 1974. In the years before World War II, Agatha Christie Mallowan—better known as simply Agatha Christie, the mystery writer—lived in Syria with her archaeologist husband. This book, which was first published the same year Syria achieved independence, tells of her experiences there.

Mannheim, Ivan. *Syria and Lebanon Handbook: The Travel Guide*. Bath, UK: Footprint Handbooks, 2001.
This travel guide offers a good overview of Syrian history and culture, as well as providing many practical facts for visitors.

Selected Bibliography

New York Times Company. *The New York Times on the Web.* 2004.
http://www.nytimes.com (November 10, 2004).
This online version of the newspaper offers current news stories along with an archive of articles on Syria.

Perthes, Volker. *Syria under Bashar al-Asad: Modernisation and the Limits of Change.* New York: Oxford University Press, 2004.
This academic study of modern Syria examines the nation's recent progress and speculates about its future.

"PRB 2004 World Population Data Sheet." *Population Reference Bureau (PRB).* 2001.
http://www.prb.org/pdf04/04WorldDataSheet_Eng.pdf (December 17, 2004).
This annual statistics sheet provides a wealth of data on Syria's population, birth and death rates, fertility rate, infant mortality rate, and other useful demographic information.

Turner, Barry, ed. *The Statesman's Yearbook: The Politics, Cultures, and Economies of the World, 2003.* New York: Macmillan Press, 2003.
This resource provides concise information on Syrian history, climate, government, economy, and culture, including relevant statistics.

Amazing Syria Guide.
http://www.syria-guide.com/indexe.htm
This website provides visitors with a wealth of information on Syrian history, geography, and culture.

BBC News. *Country Profile: Syria.*
http://news.bbc.co.uk/2/hi/middle_east/country_profiles/801669.stm
The BBC online presents an overview of Syria, complete with a timeline and links to breaking news.

Behnke, Alison, in consultation with Vartkes Ehramjian. *Cooking the Middle Eastern Way.* Minneapolis: Lerner Publications Company, 2005.
This cultural cookbook presents recipes for a variety of authentic and traditional Middle Eastern dishes, including Syrian specialties.

Café-Syria.
http://www.cafe-syria.com/
This website provides a little bit of information on almost everything related to Syria. Topics include food, cities to visit, a biography of the late president Hafez al-Assad, and much more.

Damascus Online.
http://www.damascus-online.com/index.htm
This website, which calls itself the home of "everything Syrian," presents visitors with a lengthy encyclopedia of Syrian topics, a list of common proverbs in English and Arabic, numerous photo galleries, and much more.

Davenport, John. *Saladin.* Philadelphia: Chelsea House, 2003.
This biography studies the important military and political leader Saladin.

Goldstein, Margaret J. *Israel in Pictures.* Minneapolis: Lerner Publications Company, 2004.
This book provides an overview of Israel's history and the role that it has played in the Middle East.

Katz, Samuel M. *At Any Cost: National Liberation Terrorism.* Minneapolis: Lerner Publications Company, 2004.
This book devotes a chapter to the Kurdish fight—which has sometimes included terrorism—for a homeland in the Middle East.

——. *Jerusalem or Death: Palestinian Terrorism.* Minneapolis: Lerner Publications Company, 2004.
This volume offers an introduction to the Palestinian-Israeli conflict, from its history to its ongoing violence.

Kotapish, Dawn. *Daily Life in Ancient and Modern Baghdad.* Minneapolis: Lerner Publications Company, 2000.
Explore the past and present of Baghdad, Iraq, once a capital of the Islamic Empire.

LoBaido, Anthony C., Yumi Ng, and Paul A. Rozario. *The Kurds of Asia.* Minneapolis: Lerner Publications Company, 2003.
Readers are introduced to the Kurds, a native group of Asia, with a focus on their culture and lifestyle.

Further Reading and Websites

Patterson, Charles. *Hafiz al-Asad of Syria.* Englewood Cliffs, NJ: J. Messner, 1991.
This book explores the life and career of al-Assad, Syria's president for nearly thirty years.

Ruggiero, Adriane. *The Ottoman Empire.* New York: Benchmark Books, 2003.
Explore the powerful Ottoman Empire, which ruled over Syria for more than three hundred years.

Schneider, Mical. *Between the Dragon and the Eagle.* Minneapolis: Carolrhoda Books, 1996.
This historical novel, which charts the journey of a piece of silk traded between China and the Roman Empire, takes readers through the ancient Syrian city of Palmyra.

Sherman, Josepha. *Your Travel Guide to Ancient Israel.* Minneapolis: Lerner Publications Company, 2004.
Take a fun and informative tour of ancient Israel with this book.

Syria Live.
http://www.syrialive.net/index.html
This website highlights news headlines from Syria but also provides pages on Syrian food, entertainment, and other cultural subjects.

Taus-Bolstad, Stacy. *Iraq in Pictures.* Minneapolis: Lerner Publications Company, 2004.
Offering a survey of Iraq's geography, history, and society, this book introduces readers to the nation with which Syria has often been closely involved—sometimes controversially so.

vgsbooks.com
http://www.vgsbooks.com
Visit vgsbooks.com, the homepage of the Visual Geography Series®. You can get linked to all sorts of useful online information, including geographical, historical, demographic, cultural, and economic websites. The vgsbooks.com site is a great resource for late-breaking news and statistics.

Woods, Michael, and Mary B. Woods. *Ancient Transportation: From Camels to Canals.* Minneapolis: Lerner Publications Company, 2000.
This book discusses how ancient Syrians—especially skilled Assyrian and Phoenician sailors—contributed to the technology of transportation.

Zwier, Larry, and Matthew Weltig. *The Persian Gulf and Iraqi Wars.* Minneapolis: Lerner Publications Company, 2005.
This title provides background information on Persian Gulf War of 1991, as well as the war in Iraq that has rocked the Middle East since 2003.

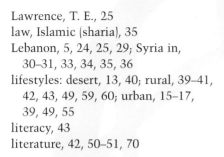

Lawrence, T. E., 25
law, Islamic (sharia), 35
Lebanon, 5, 24, 25, 29; Syria in, 30–31, 33, 34, 35, 36
lifestyles: desert, 13, 40; rural, 39–41, 42, 43, 49, 59, 60; urban, 15–17, 39, 49, 55
literacy, 43
literature, 42, 50–51, 70

al-Maarri, Abu al-Ala, 50, 51
al-Maghout, Mohammed, 51
Mamluks, 23, 24
markets (souks), 16, 17, 39
Mecca, 21, 45
Mongols, 23–24
mountains, 8, 9, 10, 13
Muawiyah, 21, 22
Muhammad (prophet), 21, 44, 45, 47
Muhammad, Usama, 55, 70
music and dance, 51–52, 71
Muslims. *See* Islam

Nasser, Gamal Abdel, 28
nomads, 13, 18, 38, 40
Nureddin, 23, 70

oil. *See* petroleum (oil)
Olympic Games, 54, 71
Organization of Petroleum Exporting Countries (OPEC), 58
Ottomans, 24–25

Palestine, 22, 23, 27. *See also* Israel
Palestine Liberation Organization (PLO), 29
Palestinians, 5, 28–29, 32, 33, 42
pan-Arabism, 25, 26, 28
Persian Gulf War, 32, 57
petroleum (oil), 15, 56–58

Qabbani, Nizar, 50
al-Qaeda, 33
Quran, 47, 48, 53

railways, 63
rainfall, 7, 9, 10, 11, 13, 59–60
Ramadan, 47–48
religions, 4, 22, 27–28, 38, 44–48; ancient, 17, 20; Christianity,

22–23, 24, 38, 47, 48, 72; Druze, 10, 25, 46; Islam, 21, 35, 38, 40, 41, 44–46, 47–48, 53; Judaism, 20, 27; Maronites, 24, 46
rivers, 9, 10, 12–13, 60; dams on, 12, 62; Euphrates, 10, 12, 60; Orontes, 10, 12, 17, 60
roads, 62–63
Roman Empire, 20–21, 71, 72

Shamma, Sara, 54, 70
Shishakli, Adib, 27, 28
Shouaa, Ghada, 54, 71
sports and recreation, 48, 54–55, 63, 71
Syria: anthem, 69; boundaries, size, and location, 4, 8; climate, 13–14; currency, 68; flag, 69; flora and fauna, 14, 15; government, 35; maps, 6, 11; population, 15, 36; topography, 8–10
Syrian Desert, 8, 10, 13, 36

television, 52, 55
terrorism, 5, 7, 29, 32, 33
Tigris-Euphrates River valley, 10, 19
Turkey, 8, 21, 22–23, 26, 38
Turkomans, 37, 38; language of, 42

Umayyad dynasty, 21–22, 23, 47
United Arab Republic (UAR), 28, 69
United Nations (UN), 27, 32, 33
United States, 32, 33, 65; sanctions of, 34, 57, 65

al-Walid, Khalid ibn, 21
wars and conflicts, 4, 56–57, 65; Arab-Israeli conflicts, 5, 8, 27, 28; ethnic, 37–38; Iran-Iraq War, 31, 56; Iraq war (2003), 7, 33–34, 37–38, 57, 65; Lebanon, 30–31, 33, 34, 35, 36; Six-Day War, 28; Syria-Israel, 27, 28, 30, 32, 33, 34, 51, 65; World War I, 25–26; World War II, 27
Wassouf, George, 51, 71
water, 15, 59–60
women, 36, 41, 43, 54, 71, 80; Islam and, 41, 54

Zangi, 23, 71
Zenobia, 71

Captions for photos appearing on cover and chapter openers:

Cover: The ruins of the Arab castle of Qalaat Jaber overlook the waters of Lake al-Assad. Like its Middle Eastern neighbors, Syria boasts many well-preserved historic sites.

pp. 4–5 The city of Aleppo is viewed at sunset with its ancient citadel on the horizon. Aleppo and the capital Damascus each claim to be the oldest continually occupied city in the world.

pp. 8–9 This view from the mountains in northwestern Syria looks down into a fertile agricultural valley.

pp. 18–19 Palmyra, an ancient city of Syria, was once an oasis on the northern edge of the Syrian Desert. However, it fell into ruin after being deserted in the third century.

pp. 36–37 A Syrian family explores the ruins of an ancient Arab castle.

pp. 44–45 Islamic women pray at the Great Mosque of Damascus. In Islam men and women worship separately.

Photo Acknowledgments

The images in this book are used with permission of: © Ed Kashi/CORBIS, pp. 4–5, 62; Ron Bell/ Digital Cartographics, pp. 6, 11; © John Elk III, pp. 8–9, 16, 29, 47, 53, 59, 64; © TRIP/Chris Rennie, p. 12; © TRIP/H. Rogers, p. 14; © Izzet Keribar, pp. 18–19, 44–45; © Art Directors/TRIP/Jane Sweeney, p. 22; © Bettmann/CORBIS, p. 26; © Maher Attar/CORBIS SYGMA, p. 31; © Reuters/CORBIS, p. 34; © Dave Bartruff/CORBIS, pp. 36–37, 40; © TRIP/Ibrahim, p. 38; © Art Directors/TRIP/Chris Rennie, p. 39; © Hanan Isachar/CORBIS, p. 46; © K. M. Westermann/CORBIS, p. 48; © Walter and Louiseann Pietrowicz/September 8th Stock, p. 49; © AFP/Getty Images, pp. 52, 54; © Christine Osborne/CORBIS, pp. 60–61; © Audrius Tomonis - www.banknotes.com, p. 68.

Cover image: © Dave Bartruff/CORBIS.

9 | 0 6 | 1